Advance Praise for *Let Go To Grow*

"Over the next ten years large companies will be hit with a wide array of harrowing new business challenges—commoditization being at the top of that list. *Let Go To Grow* elegantly outlines the critical new innovation, standardization, and globalization strategies that corporations can use to hurdle these obstacles and thrive in the coming years."

—*George F. Colony, CEO, Forrester Research, Inc.*

"This is a very important book for CEOs and top executives who are facing brutal, global competitive pressures, which is probably a majority. *Let Go To Grow* describes a strategy that will allow you as a business leader to do what you do best, while sidestepping the commoditization that's driving down profit margins in so many businesses. This book reflects not only what IBM is thinking but also what other companies, ranging from Dell to FedEx to Wal-Mart, are doing to win in extremely competitive markets. Read this book for practical real-world insights, not for any academic theories."

—*William J. Holstein, Editor-in-Chief,* Chief Executive *magazine*

"*Let Go To Grow* is a must-read for executives who are trying to use strategy and management practices to drive innovation and productivity gains. It puts concepts like componentization, outsourcing, and off-shoring in a much more strategic context than anything else I've read. The book clearly shows how winning companies have gone from optimizing value chains to managing global "value webs" for competitive advantage. The argument is enhanced significantly by specific practical case examples featuring leading companies like Dell, eBay, GE, Procter & Gamble, and Toyota."

—*Tony Friscia, President and CEO, AMR Research*

"Sanford and Taylor carefully analyze the global marketplace and offer a progressive new strategy for transforming an underperforming business....A pioneering blueprint for the 21st-century business."

—*Kirkus Reports*

LET GO TO GROW

LET GO TO GROW

ESCAPING THE
COMMODITY TRAP

Linda S. Sanford
with
Dave Taylor

PRENTICE
HALL
PTR

An Imprint of PEARSON EDUCATION
Upper Saddle River, NJ•Boston•Indianapolis•San Francisco•
New York•Toronto•Montreal•London•Munich•Paris•Madrid•
Cape Town•Sydney•Tokyo•Singapore•Mexico City

The publisher offers excellent discounts on this book when ordered in quantity for bulk purchases or special sales, which may include electronic versions and/or custom covers and content particular to your business, training goals, marketing focus, and branding interests. For more information, please contact:

U.S. Corporate and Government Sales
(800) 382-3419
corpsales@pearsontechgroup.com

For sales outside the U.S., please contact:
International Sales
international@pearsoned.com
Visit us on the Web: www.phptr.com

For information regarding permissions, write to:
Pearson Education, Inc.
Rights and Contracts Department
One Lake Street
Upper Saddle River, NJ 07458

ISBN 0-13-148208-4

Text printed in the United States on recycled paper at R.R. Donnelley in Crawfordsville, Indiana
First printing, November 2005

Library of Congress Cataloging-in-Publication Data
Sanford, Linda S.
    Let go to grow : escaping the commodity trap / Linda S. Sanford with Dave Taylor.
       p. cm.
    ISBN 0-13-148208-4
  1. Strategic planning. 2. Business planning. I. Taylor, Dave, 1962- II. Title.
    HD30.28.S265 2006
    658.4'012—dc22
                                2005022470

To IBMers worldwide, who every day, in ways both large and small, are helping our company "Let Go to Grow"

CONTENTS

3

IT'S ALL ABOUT COMPONENTS   33

4

CREATING BUSINESS COMPONENTS   47

9

ACHIEVING MEASURABLE PRODUCTIVITY IMPROVEMENTS   141

10

PRACTICAL IMPLEMENTATION OF THE COMPONENT BUSINESS MODEL   155

11
GAINING THE COLLABORATION EDGE: BUILDING THE CREATIVE COMPANY FOR THE CREATIVE ECONOMY   183

Endnotes

Index

PREFACE—
LET GO TO GROW

Sustained revenue growth is difficult. The odds of a company maintaining a growth rate above the gross national product are worse than one in ten. Markets are in such a state of flux that responding to the challenges of the marketplace with traditional business strategies does little more than let a firm survive.

This difficult business environment has been fueled by technological advances that enable suppliers and customers to work hand-in-hand, globally and in real time, remaking the way companies need to operate.

There are big winners in this economy, though. These winners are creating new opportunities by driving productivity, collaboration, and innovation in concert—through their businesses and relationships—to create a cycle of growth liberated from the vagaries of economic cycles and commoditization.

The following illustration shows what we mean.

Productivity is a driver of top-line growth, and its benefits are unmistakable.

For countries, gains in productivity spur economic growth and job creation and raise the overall standard of living. For companies, productivity drives competitiveness, offers performance bonuses and raises, and fuels long-term sustainability through acquisitions and investments in high-growth areas and new markets. Productivity is also a major factor in growth of earnings per share, a key measure of performance. Slower productivity growth or product stagnation means that companies must accept lower profit margins or raise prices, making them less competitive.

By enhancing organizational productivity with new technological and cultural advancements, time is freed up for employees, enabling them to achieve greater collaboration across the organization. This new, deep collaboration allows the organization to build teams dynamically, sparking breakthrough innovation to solve client problems.

In the 21st-century economy, innovation is a core value. Companies need to value big discoveries that open new paths for exploration and new ways to meet the ever-changing needs of the marketplace. It's not about technology (which enables all of these concepts) but about business transformation, pioneering progressive workplace policies and making a difference in the world.

Companies drive revenue growth by delivering innovation, both for their clients and for themselves. They can do this because they have built—or are building—a business based on a set of configurable components and a technology platform that gives them the ability to respond to the unpredictable and uncontrollable with speed, flexibility, and adaptability. Such leaders build value through opportunistic collaboration with clients, partners, and suppliers, choosing how to source and integrate components across their value web. They focus on profitable growth, enabled by on demand technology—available as needed, when needed, where needed—immediately integrated, open, and financially productive, not just technically efficient.

They have "Let Go to Grow."

This is a handbook for transforming your business, whether you're in the Fortune 500 or are determined to make the list.

We didn't choose the title of our book lightly. *Let Go To Grow* is all about our vision of the future of business, its implications, and our best practices. It's about the future of *your* business too.

We begin the book with some sobering marketplace realities and offer a set of management principles to guide you through the new, fluid marketplace. Chapters 3 through 8 describe the process, people, technology shifts, governance and leadership vision, qualities, and characteristics needed to succeed in this new commoditized business climate.

Chapter 9, "Achieving Measurable Productivity Improvements," explains how to measure success by driving both efficiency and growth in concert through a balanced focus on productivity, collaboration, and innovation.

The final two chapters of this book offer practical implementation details for some of our most critical ideas about componentizing your business. Chapter 11, "Gaining the Collaborative Edge: Building the Creative Company for the Creative Economy," also explains where, why, and how you can start building a Let Go to Grow business.

Let Go to Grow is not something happening in the future. It's happening right now!

We make extensive use of case studies, including GE, eBay, TAL, Dell, Toyota, Southwest, UPS, Federal Express, and IBM, to illustrate our themes and gain insight from what these innovators have recognized and created.

By understanding the principles of this book, you will gain insight into the new marketplace reality and learn how to utilize the principles collected here to drive sustained growth.

ACKNOWLEDGMENTS

We'd like to thank our family, friends, and colleagues who provided assistance, encouragement, and wisdom at all stages of this journey. We'd also like to thank all the customers we've spoken to who helped us shape and validate the ideas herein. Special thanks to Mike Zisman, Don Schulman, Peter G. W. Keen, and Ron Williams for their insight, advice, and counsel.

Thanks to Nick Donofrio and Irving Wladawsky Berger for their support and guidance and to Janet Raimondo, Marian Underweiser, Amy Thrasher, Jeff Pepper, and Bernard Goodwin for lending their expertise. Finally, special thanks goes to Greg Golden, whose dedication ensured that this book happened.

ABOUT THE AUTHORS

Linda Sanford, a senior vice president at IBM, leads IBM's internal transformation to a Let Go to Grow business. In this role, Linda is responsible for working across IBM to transform core business processes, create a platform to support those processes, and help create a culture that recognizes the value this can bring to IBM.

Previously, Linda was Senior Vice President & Group Executive, IBM Storage Systems Group, where she helped take IBM from fifth place in storage market share to second place in two years. Prior to assuming that position, Linda led IBM's global sales force, the organization that manages relationships with IBM's largest customers worldwide.

Before that, Linda was General Manager of IBM's S/390 Division, which develops, manufactures, and markets large-enterprise systems. During the early 1990s, she guided the S/390 Division through one of the most comprehensive product transformations the computer industry has ever seen, reinventing S/390 as an open, enterprise-level server.

One of the highest-ranking women at IBM, Linda is a member of the Women in Technology International Hall of Fame and the National Academy of Engineering. She has been named one of the 50 Most Influential Women in Business by *Fortune Magazine*, one of the Top Ten Innovators in the Technology Industry by *Information Week Magazine*, and one of the Ten Most Influential Women in Technology by *Working Woman Magazine*.

Linda serves on the boards of directors of ITT Industries, St. John's University, and Rensselaer Polytechnic Institute. She also serves on the Board of Directors of the Partnership for New York City and is chair of The Business Council of New York State, Inc. Linda is a graduate of St. John's University and earned an M.S. in Operations Research from Rensselaer Polytechnic Institute. She lives in Chappaqua, New York.

Dave Taylor is a lifelong entrepreneur who has been involved with both business and the Internet since 1980. He has consulted to major corporations, including Apple Computer, Sun Microsystems, IBM Corporation, and dozens of smaller entrepreneurial ventures.

The founder of four Internet startups, he has also been published more than a thousand times and has written 20 books, including *Growing Your Business with Google* (Penguin/Alpha), *Creating Cool Web Sites* (Wiley), and *Wicked Cool Shell Scripts* (NoStarch).

Dave holds an MBA from the University of Baltimore, a Masters in Education from Purdue University, and a Bachelors in Computer Science from the University of California at San Diego. A former research scientist at Hewlett-Packard's Palo Alto R&D Laboratories, he serves as an adjunct professor at the University of Colorado, Boulder, where he teaches both business and technical classes. Dave is a top-rated speaker and has cochaired a number of conferences, including the Blog Business Summit, the Future of Education Summit, and Web Marketing 2000. He has spoken or presented workshops at countless professional events, including Comdex, Networld, Internet World, and Macworld.

Dave lives in Boulder, Colorado, along with his wife, three children, two dogs, one cat, and other animals hiding in the corners. A popular blogger, Dave can be found writing about the latest business and technology topics at www.intuitive.com and www.askdavetaylor.com and can be reached via e-mail at taylor@intuitive.com.

1

GROW TO BUILD PROFITS, NOT JUST REVENUES

Deregulation, globalization, and the Internet are fueling the growth of commoditization in just about every industry. We chose our title because we believe that to grow profitably, you must let go of traditional control mechanisms and organizational practices typified by the common value "chain." Instead, you need to open up your business by building and participating in value *webs*, where value is built by a number of companies coordinating their individual capabilities to create a whole new business ecosystem.

Value webs are very different from value chains, which rely on a company's own organization and tightly controlled contracts with suppliers. Value webs are dynamic linkages across firms that adhere to four main areas of letting go:

1. Opening up the firm to source and coordinate capabilities both internally and externally, utilizing dynamic processes rather than transactions

2. Accessing specialist services even in "core" business areas

3. Creating new collaborations in research, design, manufacturing, and customer services

4. Enabling innovations by customers, suppliers, and business partners so that their growth fuels the firm's own growth and vice versa

Letting go means following these management principles.

- **Componentize your business**—Business components are re-usable, interchangeable building blocks of functions, processes, and services that may be accessed through standardized "interfaces" across your firm, offered as services or outsourced, and used to create new business configurations in such areas as supply chain management, customer service, and similar areas.

- **Integrate your components end-to-end**—Getting the components to fit together as a business platform turns commoditization from a cost problem to a growth opportunity. The platform then gives a company the ability to synchronize business components across its value webs. Supply chain management leaders, for instance, are moving closer and closer to real-time, zero inventory and on demand customer service via integration. They minimize time, waste, and overhead by integrating their processes, processes that their competitors handle on a piecemeal basis—one piece at a time, process by process.

- **Expand your growth space through collaboration**—The componentized company can use the same components in many different ways and make its platform an integral part of many value webs. How large can FedEx, UPS, and Amazon become as "companies"? They expand their value web business through new clients and partners, new services built on their componentized platforms, and the number of countries their platforms reach. The end result makes each company an integral part of a massive ecosystem, with each new value web relationship opening up yet another growth opportunity. The growth of UPS and FedEx is thus built upon the growth of their clients. UPS and FedEx grow because they're willing to share and collaborate rather than hoard and withdraw.

- **Liberate your cost structures**—Value webs enable companies to balance fixed costs with variable costs. The former come with all the risks of capital investment and lead time, whereas the variable costs—services on demand as needed, where needed, and when needed—come with lower margins but lower risks. Componentized platform companies have cost options that change the entire financial profile of growth businesses; fixed assets are no longer the driver of scale and operations, and balance sheets look very different, with far fewer fixed assets and lower working capital. Companies can now acquire capabilities, including research, manufacturing, distribution, and even product development, on a pay-as-you-need basis. These companies substitute balance sheet "assets" for value web relationships, transforming both their capital efficiency and business agility—their ability to move on demand.

Businesses should allocate their resources so that they can innovate and grow. You want your company to focus all of its efforts on these important objectives. After all, wouldn't you like the freedom to allocate more of your precious resources to drive growth rather than tread water in an increasingly competitive business ecosystem? By structuring your company into components and implementing the Let Go to Grow philosophy, you can.

- **Provide leadership that fosters innovation**—Announce the changes needed to move the company from value chain to value webs and from business functions to business components. Leaders see the changing marketplace as an opportunity to innovate and reinvent the entire company. For organizations to let go of the traditional value chain and its organizational and cultural priorities, leadership must establish the need for componentization, decentralization, appropriate centralization, and value web integration—in other words, to define and implement the organizational structure that enables growth. This transformation will not happen by accident.

- **Drive productivity**—In most companies, there is a strategic focus on either efficiency at the risk of growth or the reverse. Productivity is an invention of the Industrial Age, but post-Industrial Age companies are rapidly evolving from businesses based on hard assets to businesses based on people. For this reason, our definition of productivity needs to evolve as well. A focus solely on either revenue or cost independently is a detriment to the business. A focus on driving balance between the two—how to take your costs and use them to maximize revenue and growth—is our definition of productivity.

What if you could deliver significant growth without adding to your cost basis? For that matter, why can't you create more growth while simultaneously reducing costs? Componentized business platforms permit parallel and focused investments that accomplish both of these together.

- **Fit the pieces together**—Differentiate and integrate via governance and policies that ensure that the enterprise platform and supporting resources are in place.

We begin with the premise that commoditization is a reality. It might not be as prevalent in the space you occupy today, but if not, it will be soon. Well-run companies will always look for sources of invention and innovation but need to make commoditization an integral part of their growth capabilities instead of trying to push it away or give in to it. In many instances, value web invention and innovation turn commodities into sustained competitive advantage; that is the message from the now decades-long dominance of Wal-Mart and Southwest Airlines in businesses where just about everything is a commodity—except how growth leaders fit the pieces together.

Let Go To Grow appears at the end of one of the worst nongrowth periods in modern business history. Regrouping after several years of costcutting, price erosion, and aggressive new global competitive challengers, companies are looking to grow again, profitably. That goal will not be easy to attain, because it never has been. The odds of your company's sustaining a growth rate above that of the overall economy is less than 10 percent—regardless of its size, industry, or current status.[1]

- Of the 172 companies that appeared on the Fortune 500 list between 1955 and 1995, only 5 percent grew their revenue above the overall inflation rate.

- Just 13 percent of a sample of 1,854 companies grew consistently over a ten-year period.

- Only 16 percent of 1,008 companies tracked from 1962 to 1998 survived.

- Of the 68 companies still on the original Forbes 100 list announced in 1917, only one (General Electric) had surpassed the average return on the S&P 500.[2]

- From 1997 to 2002, the 30 firms that constitute the Dow Jones index grew less than 5 percent in revenue and gross profit and just 0.5 percent in after-tax profit. When the top 5 performers (which include Wal-Mart, Microsoft, and Merck) were subtracted, the other 25 companies had a 2.3 percent annual revenue growth and a 1.6 percent gross profit increase essentially just matching the rate of inflation.

- The average lifetime of a firm is now one-third of what it was in the 1930s; on average, large companies in North America and Europe now fail within just 20 years.[3]

The challenges of growing profits, not just revenues, are compounded by the need for every business to define its value proposition for the marketplace through differentiated components. Letting go of components that have become standardized or commoditized, focusing on those that differentiate, and integrating both is how companies will ultimately derive value.

Componentization in a Nutshell

The pressures of economics and competition drive componentization; standardized interfaces for both products and business capabilities become a requirement for efficient business and intercompany coordination. An example of the impact of componentization is the Universal Serial Bus (USB). The USB standard enabled digital cameras, scanners, PCs, printers, PDAs, external disk drives, and many other devices to connect. USB helped create the mass market for digital cameras by making it simple to link them to printers and PCs. This "open" standard—as opposed to the proprietary standards that dominated the information technology and consumer electronics fields—made the camera a component and pushed the race to commoditization. By contrast, the toner for the printer to which your camera is linked by USB is not a standardized interface but a proprietary (and very profitable) product. That is sure to change.

- Componentization rationalizes processes and fuels the growth of value webs. Cellphones are another everyday example. Early products were manufactured by such engineering-rich companies as Motorola, Ericsson, and Nokia. Now cellphones are assembled from a common set of physical components. If the physical components are the same, why can't a common interface be built so that production can be outsourced to multiple companies, exploiting the economies of scale and specialization? That is exactly what has happened. Because of standardized manufacturing interfaces, more than 60 percent of cellphones are outsourced to companies in the Electronic Manufacturing Services (EMS) industry, changing the core dynamics of the industry. A firm like Nokia, which once competed on manufacturing, now competes on design, a design that includes the blueprint for sourcing components.

- A process, activity, or business function is not a component unless it is clearly bounded and has a well-defined interface. According to the Association of American Manufacturers, only 10 percent of large manufacturing companies can process an order electronically; there is no "clean" process interface to provide a "seamless" link between processes and value web players.[4] Healthcare claim processing is an extreme example of the resulting process and administrative muddle; there is no standardized interface for handling the many different documents, codes, and plans.

- Components are more marketable when businesses perceive market value in the capabilities that the components add to their base; otherwise, components are just commodities. Supply chain leaders increasingly pick component providers that can deliver on very tight time, cost, and quality constraints. Their logistics coordinate capabilities that are in turn built on basic commodity components. This is why FedEx and UPS are no longer just package-delivery firms. Rather, they provide the components that help clients create supply chain excellence, on demand customer service, and organizational agility. A package is just a package, but FedEx and UPS are growing because of how they link the package-delivery component into clients' customer service, supply chain management, inventory management, and electronic commerce operations.

- Components get their value from applications and relationships. Realizing their potential requires a platform for synchronizing deployment and interdependencies. Business growth leaders make this their platform differentiator. Amazon is astonishing in how many ways and for how many clients and partners it extends what looks like an online shopping mall. Amazon's online infrastructure gave Toys "R" Us a strong online presence, displaying the merchandise and taking and fulfilling the order while Toys "R" Us selects the toys and manages the inventory. The Amazon infrastructure gave Borders the online capability that it could not afford to build, operate, and scale. Amazon ships an online order on Borders' e-commerce web site directly from its own fulfillment center or reserves a book for pickup at the nearest Borders store. Amazon is the platform base for innovations by many retailers seeking to get rid of excess stock. Amazon also is the free software platform for 35,000 individual programmers. "Third-party" transactions—value web links—amount to close to a quarter of Amazon's revenues and a far higher percentage of its margins. These transactions generate almost as much revenue as does Amazon's "core" business of selling books, videos, and CDs. Right from the start, Amazon's founder has always made it clear that he was building a platform with the goal of Amazon Anywhere, Anyone. Amazon spent $800 million between 1995 and 2002 to build the platform and then move to profitability.[5] It takes just months to add new value web components, such as top-quality jewelry or gourmet foods from thousands of specialty stores.

The result of componentization for the customer is commodity heaven and, for most companies, commodity hell.

Standardized interfaces enable manufacturing, services, and processes to be broken into components that can be bought, sold, integrated, and assembled on a market basis. When this process is applied mainly to the production of commodity goods, it has relatively little impact on the competitive positioning of large companies. Componentization has now moved up the knowledge and skill chain to research in pharmaceuticals, information technology development and operations, engineering, design, and administrative processes. Standardization of manufacturing platforms has become the dominant force in the car industry, and the old high-tech hardware PC, storage, server, and printer businesses are now almost entirely componentized.

Some competitive ecosystems—consumer electronics, for instance— are componentized in terms of product parts and resulting value webs utilizing Electronic Manufacturing Services providers. Others, such as telecommunications, have resulted in a phone call being a component that can be handled by just about any standard network, with payment through prepaid phone cards or internationally via such free Internet "peer-to-peer" services as Skype (note the term "free"). In retailing, Wal-Mart and other supply chain maestros force componentization and standardized interfaces throughout their supply chains. Amazon has used standardized interfaces to precious-gem providers to make this previously well-guarded, high-markup retail specialization— jewelry sales—into another component of its catalog and its customer service platform. As for manufacturing, Asia has become the component provider to the world, and prices dropped by a fifth in five years.

Componentization takes time and cost out of the customer-delivery chain—time to market, manufacture, distribute, and service—and the cost of parts, labor, inventory, and overhead. But it does so only for a relatively small number of firms, whose experiences provide the basis for the recommendations that we present in our book. The good news for those growth leaders who create a business platform to coordinate components and synchronize their deployment inside and outside the company is that they create a significant advantage over their median competitors in key financial metrics: overhead, working capital, and margins in particular.

Componentizing businesses also enables key processes to become at least one time unit faster: What took a week is now done in days, and multiday processes now take hours. Most critical of all is that years become months, which creates a sustainable growth edge in design, new-product innovation, global competition, response to customer demand, and shifts in taste and preferences. One measure of the beneficial impact of the componentization and integration of supply chains is that the fraction of U.S. gross domestic product tied up in logistics dropped from 16.2 percent to 8.7 percent between 1980 and 2003.

The bad news for the laggards is that they become commodity companies, with a corresponding loss of product and service differentiation and the inability to maintain prices or pass on production price increases to customers, including the increased costs of fuel, raw materials, and employee benefits. The coming decade will see an increase in costs without companies, being able to raise consumer prices commensurately.

Increases in costs used to mean increases in prices. Now it is more likely to mean erosion of margins. Airlines saw fuel costs reach record levels in 2004, and although prices did not keep up, competitive intensity certainly did. The chairman of one major carrier stated that 70 percent of its customers now have a choice of a low-cost airline on its routes, compared to 14 percent in 1990. Airline customers switch if there is price differential of even $5. When several major carriers announced a $10 fuel surcharge, other airlines rejected the price increase, undermining the move.

Costs do not determine prices in competitively intensive, open markets. To customers with choices, your cost is your problem, not theirs. Cost inflation only makes the commodity player's plight even worse. An unexpected bottleneck in the global supply chain, for example, can suddenly create a cost jump. China's construction boom in 2004 led to the cost of shipping coal and metals tripling, and tanker capacity could not match demand. Australian coal prices could not increase, though production idle time increased as mines sat for days at a time waiting for ships to become available.

Cost inflation will become a major problem if the cost of basic materials increases. The trend is ominous for firms in commodity hell. The spot price for hot-rolled band steel—a key component in construction, kitchen appliances, and many other products—fell from $352 a ton in 1994 to $210 in 2002.[6] In June 2004, it hit a peak price of $590.

The business press in mid-2004 cheerfully announced that for the first time in years, businesses might regain their ability to increase prices. Industry optimists who thought that they would regain some modicum of price control jumped from 2 percent of CEOs surveyed in 2003 to 22 percent in 2004. More than three-quarters of the executives surveyed remain pessimists. Inflation will not help lift their hopes, because price increases are not margin increases in an inflationary economy. Nor are revenue increases profit enhancements. Even in good times, revenue growth may not turn into profits. That is one of the lessons of the dot-com era. Markets today are in such a state of flux that traditional business strategies produce a firm built to survive, not one built to grow.

Commoditization pushes firms to be reactive, not proactive, in their business strategies, and they struggle to regain control. Growth leaders handle global sourcing as a proactive opportunity to add capabilities, whereas other companies respond with cost-slashing survival tactics. Componentization then continues to put pressure on them and increases commoditization, a truly debilitating cycle.

Growth in and of itself is not necessarily the answer. Fewer than half of all mergers and acquisitions create shareholder value, yet M&A is one of the most widely used vehicles for generating growth. Even in good times, sustaining growth is the exception, not the rule. Growth also produces a massive up-front penalty, loosely termed "restructuring costs." Until recent changes in accounting rules, these costs did not show up as reductions in operating profits and could be allocated as "extraordinary" items on the income statement. When these costs become ordinary, they are a burden paid in advance for the opportunity to grow, without any guarantee of success. There are many examples of firms that have incurred restructuring costs of $500 million to $1 billion by writing down fixed assets that are no longer seen as strategic contributors to the firm or because of the impact of M&As on operations and staffing.

One of the most important contributions of value webs to business agility is the cost optionality it permits. The previously mentioned companies—and most of the rest of the Fortune 1000—frequently need to jettison fixed-cost burdens so they can move ahead. Let Go to Grow companies can move more quickly and without being trapped carrying the burden of so many fixed-cost balance sheet items. Cost optionality requires componentization, however, because if a process or a product does not have a standardized interface, there is no option other than keeping it in-house.

Companies need options in cost structures, capability sourcing, scaling of operations, and relationships. The challenges of managing costs and growth are daunting at the strategic and operational levels of the business. In good times, business strategy can reduce the reliance on cost stability, but the first years of this new century have not allowed any large company to coast along; management vigilance, governance, and focus on execution remain critical.

Don't give up hope, however! There are still very big winners in this new and dynamic economy. *Let Go To Grow* distills their experiences into practical management principles that will improve your chances of building and sustaining growth at better than the historical average of 10 percent. These firms consistently and profitably drive very rapid growth. They grow in bad times and in good times. They innovate on an everyday basis and are highly cost-efficient. In the most commoditized industries, they find new process and service innovations. They grow their revenues and profits with relatively little increase in capital investment or organizational size.

How they accomplish these goals is the topic of our book, a 21st-century business construction manual for executives. *Let Go To Grow* is a guide to creating a business structure and set of organizational configurations explicitly focused on growing your company continuously and profitably through the componentization transformation. What stands out among business leaders is not that they have any specific strategic insight or proprietary advantage or common business model but rather that they *configure* their organizations to link strategy to execution. They view their businesses at all levels and across all operational areas as a *platform* built on a set of components: building blocks that turn business functions, activities, and processes into capabilities that can be mobilized, linked, shared, reused, and coordinated instead of simply carried out. They reject the value chain model, which was built on in-house operations and tight control, to create roles in value webs—a structure enabled by componentization, where the key value is the ability to coordinate components, integrate them with other players' platforms, and synchronize services and processes in realtime.

A few examples of such companies and how they exploit componentization are listed next. In later chapters, we examine how these leaders have built to grow. These examples give you just a hint of the growth opportunities created by leveraging componentization:

- **GE**—By centralizing and standardizing process components globally, GE has moved many of its administrative and overhead functions to a Lego-block approach. GE is building what we call a Coordination value web, a synchronized orchestration of relationships and on demand services.

- **eBay**—The company is a platform for a wide community of large and small players to add their own services and capabilities to the overall business offering. These services range from reverse logistics (auctioning of retailers' returned goods) to government auctions and auction brokers. As an Enabling value web, the eBay platform offers new opportunities for innovation and invention.

- **TAL**—This Hong Kong apparel firm coordinates hundreds of factories, shippers, and other players in a global value web that enables retailers to order goods on demand in small units and with minimum inventory. It is a massive Services value web in an industry that gets more and more componentized by the year, while TAL gets more and more profitable.

- **Cemex**—The Cemex Way coordinates nine major business components that can be moved into new acquisitions within weeks and has helped the firm grow to number 3 in the cement industry (from 35th in the early 1980s) and to be by far the most profitable player in the world. It has made component coordination its strategic edge in customer service, manufacturing, and international operations. Cemex was one of the first transnational firms to recognize that the information technology platform is not "systems" but the core vehicle for the coordination of people.

- **P&G**—This old-line firm reinvented itself, creating a new style of operations that included componentizing its previously closely guarded portfolio of patents by licensing them to competitors on a royalty basis. Now every P&G patent is available for license to any outsider as long as that patent has existed for at least five years or has been in use in a P&G product for at least three years, whichever comes first. P&G has replaced its tight control of in-house operations and now expects half its product innovations to come from outside the firm.[7]

- **BMW**—The top-of-the-line carmaker does not make or assemble any of the parts of its popular X3 sports utility vehicle. Magna Steyr handles this on a contract-manufacturing basis, saving BMW a billion dollars in plant investment and avoiding a five-year delay in releasing the car to market. By making car manufacturing a variable cost, BMW reduces its risks and is able to focus more on design, marketing, and sales.

- **FedEx and UPS**—These former package-delivery companies have become the logistics arm, shipping department, and distributor for a vast number of other firms. Why should other companies build facilities and invest capital when these two companies can handle repairs, inventory management, and even financial services?

Growth comes from letting go and moving from control to value web relationships. The business platform, leadership, and governance principles of these firms allow them to fit the components together in new ways rather than have to invent new pieces in-house or expand existing ones. This integration of components lets them thrive in the on demand world of faster, cheaper, better. Uncertainty, change, and risk become their ally, not the enemy they are for companies that are built only to survive.

Leaders exploit their componentization capabilities and choose how to source their value options, opportunistic collaboration with clients, suppliers, and partners. Leaders may decide to outsource components, offer them as a value web service, cosource them through tight collaborations, or configure them in completely new ways. There is no one best option here. The key point is that Let Go to Grow companies have choices that traditional value chain companies lack. Let Go to Grow means "welcome to the options economy"—options on sourcing, cost structures, relationships, and scale.

Growth without profits is a gamble, one that so many dot-coms took in the hope that growth would create revenues that would eventually create profits. In contrast, Let Go to Grow companies focus on profits right from the start. They can move quickly and flexibly to locate and integrate the next profitable opportunity. They manage their cost structures via cost "optionality," the choice of variable versus fixed costs and expense versus capital, with an emphasis on external process assets instead of internal operations. By focusing beyond their own value chain, they target value webs where they also share in partners' growth. This is the capability-driven, relationship-adept, agile firm that is built to grow regardless of the economy, industry, and competition.

These companies are also technology enabled. Their modular componentization, ability to build collaborative and integrated value webs, and cost optionality opportunities allow responsiveness to markets, customers, and environmental shifts. This is what we call *on demand*, "as and when needed or opportune" but also "end-to-end across processes, partners, and services" and "most productively and cost-effectively." All of these capabilities require on demand technology: available as, when, and where needed, immediately integrated, and financially productive, not just technically efficient. A componentized business needs componentized technology. For every business characteristic of letting go to grow, there must be a corresponding technology equivalent: agility, cost variability, speed, opportunistic collaboration, relationships, and end-to-end integration.

It is only in the past few years that this correspondence between business strategy and technology has become practical and scalable for even large-scale operations. Although it is management principles that define Let Go to Grow, this new set of technology platforms and tools are a vital underpinning of on demand, synchronized value webs.

In providing examples of these principles and platforms in action, the opening chapters of our book answer the question, Is this for real? and respond with a never-ending, Yes, it is. This is not a theoretical business strategy book but the very immediate present for just about any industry. Right now, industry leaders are driving up their profits even where their margins are under pressure, whereas the built-to-survive players continue to face revenue erosion and respond with never-ending cycles of cost cutting. The growth experts create new premium capabilities, products, and services through their value webs, leaving the commodity-only players trapped competing on price alone. They use the new global on demand talent base of process and service providers to build tightly integrated and perfectly synchronized value webs while their competitors outsource based on cost with no real advantage or value for themselves, their clients, or their business partners.

It is time for you to join these leaders, for your organization to accelerate the pace and scale of your value web creation and relationships. Don't look back; your competitors will be running in place. Look forward and make sure that you move to the front of the race—one of the pacesetters.

Summary

Growing your business in this new century is going to require that you let go of traditional control mechanisms, give up on value chains, and instead move your company to a new way of thinking about your place in your business ecosystem. It's what we call a value *web*, and it allows value to be built by a consortium of coordinating firms pooling their capabilities and resources.

2

COMMODITY MARKETS DEFINED

W here are the growth engines for businesses today? How do firms avoid the commoditization that is occurring across so many industries? The answer may surprise you: *Commoditization forces the growth engine* and is the ally of the growth business, though it will remain the enemy of the fixed-structure company. It's time to reinvent your organization.

Here are the modern realities of business:

Profitable growth is difficult

It has always been difficult to build profitable growth and even more difficult to sustain a profitable growth path. Only a tiny fraction of firms have *ever* succeeded in doing so. The pragmatic reality is that most long-term business growth barely keeps up with economic growth, and revenue increases hover around the national inflation rate.

And getting exponentially more difficult

Even if you're managing to keep up with the ever-increasing pace of competition, it is getting exponentially more difficult to grow profitably as the interaction of deregulation, globalization, and Internet-based technology fuels more and more competitive intensity. This is not a linear evolution but a compounded and accelerating steep curve. Each of these critical forces fuels competition; globalization of manufacturing and labor, Internet-enabled electronic commerce, Internet-enabled supply chain management, and the deregulation of telecommunications are obvious instances.

When these changes interact and feed on one another, entire competitive ecosystems lose their traditional identity and levers of control. At this point, there are very few industries that are not being reshaped by these changes, forced through the stages of creative destruction. Telecommunications, travel services, consumer electronics, auto manufacturing, computers, banking, software, and the music business have all been reinvented in the past decade. In some instances, deregulation is the pivot; telecommunications is the most obvious instance. In others, it is globalization, as in consumer electronics and auto manufacturing. In still others, the Internet subverts the status quo; travel services are an example. Once any of these forces gains critical mass, the others come into play, creating a new level of competitive intensity that accelerates. Almost inevitably, the three forces converge at some point; the Internet is in many ways part of the globalization of labor supply and in itself a form of deregulation in its removal of protective barriers to entry, control of channels, and constraints on the flow of information on prices and services.

The Ecosystem Impact

The impact of these forces on the ecosystem is inevitable: overcapacity, customer power (which translates fairly immediately to price competition), and then componentization as a necessary response and commoditization as the inevitable outcome. These all interact, too. They feed back into the environment of globalization, deregulation, and technology; this is demonstrated by the competitive intensity of the consumer electronics ecosystem—manufacturers, supply chain services, contract manufacturers, designers, retailers, electronic commerce portals, and fabrication plant giants. This used to be a high-tech industry. Now, it is a commodity ecosystem characterized by overcapacity, customer power, componentization, and thus continually shrinking margins and price cuts.

The interaction of all these new competitive changes also produces a system of continual innovation in technology, methods, and services. Because these are rapidly componentized and incorporated into the products of all the main players in the mass market, the innovations themselves end up pushing these companies toward commoditization. Digital cameras, computer storage, mobile phones, and PDAs exemplify the breakneck pace of innovation and commoditization.

As competition intensifies, overcapacity grows. Technology generates competition; so does deregulation. Globalization adds to it. For example, China and India are fueling competition around the world by offering low-cost services and products. Customer power increases as a direct result of deregulation, compounded by the degree to which the Internet provides customers with information and new choices. When customer power is constrained by regulation, options are limited because of market protectionism, and information on services and prices carefully protects providers, the customer ends up at the end of the industry value "chains." When customers learn how to pick and choose, they go for the best deal and increasingly know where to find it. Ecosystems reshaped by the deregulation globalization Internet combination of forces have seen prices drop at least 20 percent over a five-year period; telecommunications, air fares, consumer electronics, and, more recently, prescription drugs are leading examples.

The Ecosystem Response

The response to increased competitive intensity is componentization: the move to interchangeable parts. As carmakers, PC hardware product brands, and financial service firms respond to competitive intensity, they focus on cost efficiency. They abandon their in-house manufacturing and proprietary parts and seek out low-cost suppliers that can provide off-the-shelf resources. These resources increasingly also include off-the-shelf processes, such as customer service, back-office functions, distribution, and supply chain management. The Internet becomes the enabling vehicle for collaboration in componentized engineering, design, and research.

For all this to be efficiently managed, low cost, quality, and speed are essential. Companies in the mainstream of the ecosystem have no choice but to move toward standardized interfaces: shared agreements, some specific and some implicit, on how components link together. For instance, customers can now add more memory to their PCs without going through the manufacturer: They walk into a store like Best Buy or run a search on Google and quickly pick their best option. The component providers offer different prices and vary the details of their products, but their components interface directly to the PC.

Componentization Drives Commoditization

Low-cost producers look for advantages of scale, and specialist players tailor their strategies to standardized interfaces. Going back to the example of PC memory, have you ever heard of Kingston? Look at the ads in your newspaper and you'll see that merchants now emphasize low-price components (including Kingston, just one of the commodity players). From a commoditization perspective, contract manufacturers, such as Flextronics, are why your printer, PDA, or digital camera costs less than it did six months ago; they are all built on componentized parts assembled through standardized interfaces to create branded products. HP is among the best-known printer brands, yet it has outsourced all manufacturing, and repairs are handled exclusively by UPS.

When you call a company for customer service or technical assistance, are you reaching a site in Ireland, India, or Omaha? Call centers are now viewed as a business component. So, too, are more and more manufacturing, back-office, and other previously in-house capabilities. How many hospital patients know that their X-rays and MRIs are sent directly to Makati in the Philippines? How many of the standard parts in an "American" or a "Japanese" car were made in the home country? Do customers need to know?

Competitive intensity creates ecosystem impact, and commoditization is the inevitable outcome. There will always be a space for the innovator to invent something truly "new." But commoditization catches up quickly. "New" quickly becomes "standard," which soon becomes "special price," which then begets free printer, installation, or two for the price of one. Mortgages, computer storage, hotel rooms, medications, airplane tickets, mobile phone services: The list is long, and no ecosystem is immune to this commoditization drift.

Commodity Heaven and Hell

Commodity hell for producers is commodity heaven for customers. They pick channels, providers, and products on whatever basis they want, in complete control of the transaction. Customers may not necessarily choose on the basis of price; the key is that they have choices. In some instances, the choice favors design, or fashion is the deciding factor, and they will pay a little more for the same commodity functionality of, say, a printer or a mobile phone. They will in other instances favor a brand for a different reason.

In many cases, the owner of the brand may have little to do with the production, delivery, and servicing of the goods. One illustrative example is Hong Kong-based TAL Group, the coordinator of a value web that such retailers as JC Penney and Lands' End use to produce customized dress shirts. JC Penney takes the order in the store, and TAL does the rest, synchronizing hundreds of raw materials providers, factories, and shippers to deliver as small an order as one shirt, with the appropriate logo sewn on, to JC Penney or even direct to the customer. TAL accounts for one in eight of all the dress shirts sold in the United States, but it is doubtful that their purchasers have ever heard of the firm. The customer gets a customized shirt at a commodity price. TAL is an instance of how coordination of value webs can help firms escape from commodity hell. They offer a services web that firms like JC Penney utilize as an extension of their value chain to create a new degree of coordination.

> *It is coordination of value web capabilities that drives every growth leader.*

The General Response: Tighten Control

The typical ecosystem reaction to commodity hell is control centered: Try to get on top of the changes. This "tighten control" strategy centers on cost cutting, outsourcing, efficiency, mergers and acquisitions, and restructuring. There is a truly hellish catch here, though: Control fuels the very forces that created the need for control in the first place, creating a terrible feedback loop (as depicted in Figure 2.1).

Welcome to the Cruel Economy.

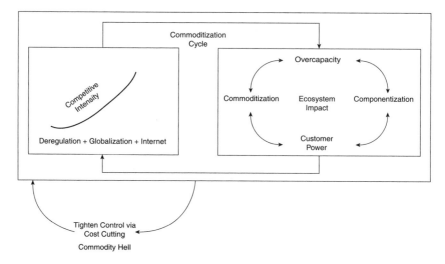

Figure 2.1 Commoditization cycle.

The Alternative: Let Go to Grow

There is an alternative response to commodity hell: an on demand business platform that we characterize as Let Go to Grow. The winners in creating and sustaining growth in the era of commoditization will profit and thrive by putting the pieces together in new ways and by changing their traditional thinking.

The term "platform" is used in many contexts, but it is fundamentally a foundation, launch pad, and set of standardized interfaces. A business platform is essentially a set of business capabilities on which other capabilities can be built, linked, and expanded to meet the pace of customer demand and relationship needs. In the technology world, a platform is a set of technologies on which other technologies are built. Windows is a software platform on which thousands of applications are built and linked. Microsoft was able to leverage Windows through its market might, but it appears that the company is seeing Linux, backed by IBM and a number of other players, as an increasing threat. The Linux platform provides similar capabilities but in a more open development arena, using open standards that have, through the inevitable forces described in this book, enabled Linux to take a significant foothold. Similarly, Intel's individual products constitute the core hardware platform of the PC ecosystem. In the car industry, standardized manufacturing platforms have replaced independent model designs and facilitated reuse of components, global coordination of designs and production. In financial services, the credit card is a platform on which entirely new payment services have been developed. Through its links to a wide range of processing capabilities, the credit card has also been extended into non-credit areas. For example, credit cards now enable automated check-in at airports; the airline uses this standardized identification in a completely nonfinancial manner.

The Business Platform

A business platform has three distinct elements:

- **Governance rules and roles**—Components are individual; a platform is designed for coordination and collaboration. Successful platforms require policies with teeth—governance rules—and allocation of authority and responsibility that ensures enterprise coordination *plus* localized application and innovation.

- **Blueprints and interface standards**—The degree of linkage, extension, and collaboration rests on technology standards, industry practices, and process interfaces.

- **Integration capabilities**—A platform coordinates many players in value webs and must be able to grow in reach, range, and robustness. *Reach* refers to the link with customers and partners; *range*, to the variety of roles a platform can play and services it can offer or support; *robustness*, to end-to-end quality and reliability.

The air traffic control system is a splendid illustration of these three platform elements. Governance rules and roles are the glue of ATC: its regulatory framework. The individual passenger is largely unaware that components, generating flight operations, check-in procedures, terminal operations, and facilities rely on these rules. ATC includes many blueprints to ensure coordination of components. The entire system must manage 5,000 planes in U.S. air space at any one time and synchronize all the many interactions this involves.

Let Go To Grow is an executive handbook for defining the business equivalent of the air traffic control system: your firm's business platform. Agility is the key to profitable growth in commodity hell. It breaks the negative feedback loop of the "tighten control" strategy and creates options for growth.

We titled our book *Let Go To Grow* because letting go is the key management and cultural shift necessary to grow, to become a firm that combines speed, flexibility, adaptability, coordination, collaboration, and innovation. The role of the business platform is to enable growth, and the role of the corporate culture is to exploit the opportunities that the platform enables.

We base our analysis on an in-depth review of firms that have successfully made the shift to become agile firms—our work is not at all hypothetical. Although these leaders are very different in size, industry, strategy, and other ecosystem demographics, they show the same overall drive for growth. They accept commoditization and use their platforms as an ally. Wal-Mart and Dell sell commodity goods, and their supply chains are the coordination of components. GE's governance rules componentize its back-office and administrative processes across its many diverse units. This GE standardization creates, rather than blocks, innovations in organizational design and location.

Growth leaders let go of the traditional value chain and build relationships everywhere, relying on partners for capabilities that used to be protected as "core" and kept in-house. They turn outsourcing of functions into insourcing of capabilities, drawing on collaborations in design, engineering, and distribution that they bring in-house even though outside parties handle them.

They grow through others' growth. UPS handles close to two-thirds of all online e-commerce transactions. Its ads speak of its "synchronizing" its customers' entire logistics, from warehousing to shipping to inventory management to financing. UPS gives up control to its customers in order to build growth, and in doing so, it fuels its partners' profitable growth by providing logistical expertise, scale, and systems without the partner firms' needing to make heavy investments of capital, organization, and people.

Growth leaders make the truisms about commitment to the customer a reality. They give up control of information and decision-making to the customer and facilitate customer innovation via their own platforms. Amazon's platform synchronizes a set of components that even competitors like Borders use. Some 35,000 e-commerce technology developers use the Amazon technology platform as they want. Amazon associates are any person, company, club, public-sector group, or school anywhere that would like to earn commissions through connecting its customers to Amazon. FedEx gives customers complete control of their interactions with the company—FedEx gives up control to gain collaboration and growth. Similarly, eBay is *explicitly*, not accidentally, driven by its customers; eBay grows and grows as a result.

Above all, business-platform leaders are leaders because top management understands the platform issues. That is of critical importance to moving from component hell into platform-driven growth. Platforms rest above all on governance rules. Spot the component/commoditization trends early, and take charge of change.

Commoditization: Enemy or Opportunity?

Commoditization is a scary word for most executives. Given that we are living in an era in which commoditization of entire industries is the main trend, the term will inevitably become even scarier, and commoditization will force many companies into a struggle for survival. The automotive business is one example of an industry in which every company used to be a confederation of separate design and production facilities, manufacturing specifications, and car models built of entirely different parts. Now, survival rests on componentization: shared designs and manufacturing production lines, tight coordination of multiple supply chain relationships, standard parts, and skilled use of specialist suppliers.

Many players in this ecosystem are struggling. The secret to making commoditization an ally is a statement by an executive in Timken, the century-old maker of bearings: "There are factories around the world that are focusing on one simple product, and they're killing us on price."[1] The key now, he says, is to surround the company's basic product with additional components in order to provide customers with exactly what they want.

The On Demand Business has a platform in place—policies, governance rules, and process and technology blueprints—to exploit componentization as an integrative opportunity. Many automakers and parts suppliers have not been able to create such a platform, however. They get all the disadvantages of componentization and see few of its benefits. Parts makers see prices fall and fall. Carmakers see platform leaders ahead of them in time to market, manufacturing cost and flexibility, and supply chain efficiency. The business-platform leaders, most obviously Toyota, push componentization—and hence commoditization—of their suppliers farther and faster. They push innovation and end-to-end business integration equally farther and faster.

Large companies in all industries are moving to exploit the advantages of componentization wherever possible. Many of them were operating on the very opposite principle of componentization—overreliance on in-house capabilities in every area of business. Procter & Gamble is an example of a company making the shift. P&G has opened up its boundaries and componentized many in-house operations, giving them added flexibility and options. Componentization has also affected how P&G operates as a supplier: Wal-Mart has handed over inventory management in its stores to P&G and made it the "category captain"[2] for all detergents, regardless of manufacturer, sold at Wal-Mart.[3]

These are outside relationships to be coordinated rather than operations to be run internally.

In the pharmaceutical industry, research and development is being componentized through linkages to outside teams, patent licensing, and project outsourcing. Research hospitals, such as St. Jude in Memphis, Tennessee, now have their own small manufacturing plant to take their experimental products into small-scale production. They then invite large pharmaceutical firms to take over full production and marketing. Biocon in India has 300 research scientists working on an outsourcing contractual basis with such firms as Pfizer. R&D is rapidly moving from an in-house preserve to componentized collaboration—a value web of synchronized relationships.

Competitive necessity is forcing this opening up of boundaries. Componentization is the logical result of pressures to reduce costs, simplify and standardize processes, and speed up operations. Overcapacity, global competition, and technology combine to fuel the move toward standardization of how components link to one another. The individual parts may be different, but they can be assembled through the same interfaces. Buyers then look to obtain the most cost-effective elements, the ones that offer the best quality, or those that can be used in multiple products. Large buyers are in a position to make high demands, especially on price, because the interface enables them to switch to another provider of a component without any retooling or manufacturing down time.

Componentization decomposes traditional value chains. Instead of relying on in-house resources, companies now increasingly look to use components from a wide range of suppliers and allies. They rationalize internal operations, with outsourcing often a decision made on economic necessity. In the auto industry, shared manufacturing platforms replace independent design and production facilities. In the consumer electronics and personal computer markets, the leading brands focus their skills on design even though they outsource all manufacturing to a company that assembles their product out of standard components.

The pressures of commoditization increase componentization in all areas. Many of the recent innovations of old-economy leaders, such as GE and Toyota, and new-economy growth firms, such as eBay and Amazon, are the result of their leaders' aggressive focus on componentizing internal processes so that they can be standardized, reused across the company, and made the basis for entirely new organizational structures, customer services, and partnerships. These firms innovate in supply chain management, fine-tuning their operations to a degree that every major relationship requires on demand synchronization of components, with their quality and service demands, but not the prices they pay, ever increasing.

In the information technology field, componentization is transforming the entire industry. Historically, just about every key element of IT was "proprietary"; there were few interchangeable parts, and each major software, hardware, and telecommunications provider had its own closed systems. This proprietary era is rapidly coming if not to a close, at least to a standstill. IT is becoming fully componentized through standardized interfaces: tools and services for linking documents, applications, and data items regardless of their technology base. Microsoft and Apple are the two remaining proprietary players in an industry in which all the key acronyms mean "components": Linux, XML, USB, and Web Services, to name just a few.

IBM made a shift in the same direction as P&G several years ago, toward increased reliance on open standards in lieu of proprietary systems and products. Proprietary interfaces are the past of IT and in only a few cases—as with Windows—are still a major factor in the present. Standardized open interfaces are IT's future. Although this is commoditizing many previously highly paid IT skills through global sourcing, the componentization that it brings is transforming the costs, speed, quality, and flexibility of IT—at last! One of the most powerful impacts of IT componentization is its on demand capabilities; it has enabled new linkages to instantly coordinate global value web operations.

The Business Platform as Growth Engine

Some firms extend the marketable value of their components and make them an integral part of value webs. UPS and FedEx offer their logistics components to enable new capabilities in customer service and supply chain management. Referring back to the Timken executive's comment about surrounding basic products with additional components, FedEx and UPS surround their basic shipping with warehousing, management of repairs, freight consolidation, and many other services. What makes these "components" is that they are interchangeable with clients' own services and systems. UPS and FedEx are a portfolio of assembly blocks that customers can add to their own business platforms.

Such linkable components become multidimensional capabilities that are of value in many contexts and partnerships. They can be the basis for profitable business expansion, because componentization transforms the dynamics and costs of growth. This approach also opens up new options for sourcing by offering variable costs and on demand services instead of fixed capital investment, with all its risks and lead times. It creates opportunities to make components the building blocks of new value webs—cross-organizational complexes, such as the global coordination machine that TAL has built to synchronize clothes manufacturing with hundreds of partners, and the automotive contract manufacturing company Magna to which BMW has outsourced the entire production of its X3 series of SUVs.

Amazon reuses its components to build profitable relationships with any web site owner, thousands of independent software developers, several of its competitors, and many retailers. Amazon is built on its business platform. The power of componentization is illustrated by the personal announcement in April 2004 by its chairman, Jeff Bezos, that Amazon was entering the jewelry market. He stated that he could buy a jewel wholesale for $500 and sell it online, with guarantees of a high-quality product, for $575. Tiffany and Zales sell the same stone for $1,000. Amazon has the technology platform in place, the catalog management system, ordering and order fulfillment, and shipping—a value web component provided by UPS and the U.S. Postal Service—to allow this dramatic improvement in efficiency.[4]

There is a consistent pattern in the strategies of leaders like Jeff Bezos of Amazon, Jeff Immelt of GE, Meg Whitman of eBay, Michael Dell of Dell Computer, Fred Smith of FedEx, Sam Palmisano of IBM, and many smaller firms. It is the commitment to the business platform as the edge in a component world. Without that commitment at the top, governance is missing, and the company ends up as the sum of its (often) commoditizing parts. As those parts lose value, so too does the firm.

Making the Platform a Success

Componentization and commoditization are your enemy *unless* you have the platform to turn a commodity business into a growth engine. That takes speed, flexibility, adaptability, coordination, collaboration, innovation, and cost optionality:

- **Speed of deployment**—*Move fast*: Reuse a component, link it to a business partner, sell it as a service, source it as a new capability.

- **Flexibility**—*Move nimbly*: Add components from partners, extend your value webs, fine-tune your supply chain.

- **Adaptability**—*Move in good time*: Source new components for new situations and business opportunities.

- **Coordination**—*Move together*: Link components via the platform; use IT as the coordination and synchronization base for complex processes and webs.

- **Collaboration**—*Create together*: Build new capabilities for yourself and partners via existing components and as part of new services and relationships.

- **Innovation**—*Invent opportunistically*: Continuously look to extend and create value webs; innovate on behalf of the customer.

- **Cost optionality**—*Earn as you go and grow*: Turn long lead time, high-risk capital investments, and fixed costs into variable costs; scale on demand.

Components plus a platform give you options. Options drive growth opportunity. Components without a platform equal not very much for your company's future options!

Future business historians may view componentization as the key to growth in a new century. Their response to the commoditizing impact of componentization is akin to judo, not boxing. In judo, you stop fighting your opponent and go with the flow. Leverage componentization for your advantage, not your opponent's. The challenge is to use components to not get stuck with just components.

What's Left When Everything Is Just a Component?

Logically, if an entire industry ends up componentized, the product must become just a commodity. In many instances, that clearly is the case. The personal computer industry is an obvious example. It moved from high tech to commodity in just a few years. It is now a component business. But no matter how commoditized the industry, there is always a space for effective differentiation, as demonstrated by the ongoing success of Apple Computer.

Others find their space in the component economy by using their business platforms to extend the capabilities of customers and partners. Auto parts manufacturer American Axle and Manufacturing is, in its founder's words, "transforming Detroit into a low-cost country"[5] (making a $170 million profit on $3.7 billion in sales in 2003). It found its place in GM's manufacturing webs and augments component parts with an IT platform that coordinates quality management and metrics. Magna allows BMW to totally outsource entire model lines, as Magna also has for Saab and Mercedes, through its coordination of planning and design and its expertise in production engineering.

In the equally distressed electronics parts market, Flextronics "bundles" components on behalf of major computer "manufacturers," helping them customize their products. Flextronics provides standard outsourcing for brand-name consumer electronics manufacturers, and its revenues are bigger than most of theirs; its edge is its reliability and ability to operate with an overhead of only 2 percent to 4 percent. These relationships are platform to platform, not transaction buyer to seller.

Componentized products, processes, and services make design and supply chain management their growth and profit advantage. If you walk through a Best Buy or Circuit City store, your choice of a computer printer or a digital camera is likely to be based on brand, but you can be almost certain that the vendor outsourced the manufacturing and product distribution. HP is best known for its printers. It designs and markets them but makes none of them; manufacturing is completely outsourced.

The New Service Providers in the Component Economy

Let Go To Grow is for corporate executives and their advisers who must shape their companies' strategic positioning. Our focus is thus mostly on how to build flexibility. Part of that rests on finding such suppliers and partners as Magna, UPS, Flextronics, IBM, and other on demand service providers, whether they are to be found in-house or at third-party firms.

The chairman of Flextronic boasts that one key capability his firm's platform offers is the ability to move production of a model from, say, China to Mexico, in three weeks. This makes Flextronic rather different in profile from its customers. The company relies on scale and absorbs much of the fixed cost and risks of operations.

For example, BMW orders X3 SUV production from Magna on an as-needed, pay-on-demand basis. Magna saves BMW from investing a billion dollars in a new facility. But Magna has to spend its own money on building capacity. In the IT field, more and more services are being offered on the same basis: on demand and with variable cost. The providers must have many of the characteristics of utilities: scale, reliability, financial capital strength, and a strong reputation. If that were all they had, however, they'd still be trapped in the commodity economy. They would be offering components on a price basis. Instead, the leaders are all building strong business platforms, emphasizing their integration rather than their individual component offerings, and adopting standardized interfaces.

IBM's business strategy is built around this concept of on demand. Components and on demand are obviously interrelated; one implies the other. But the key to making them powerful forces for growth is the business platform: linking user to supplier platform and adding more and more dimensions of value beyond the transaction price of the component.

Summary

Growth is difficult, and there's no reason to think that it's going to get any easier to produce profitable growth in your market segment, regardless of what it is. Among the forces causing this are deregulation, globalization, and the pervasiveness of the Internet and high-speed global communications. These are producing continual innovation while simultaneously forcing commoditization. The response? Componentization, which makes value webs such a powerful and critical part of your future business strategy.

3

IT'S ALL ABOUT COMPONENTS

What are business components? What happens to an industry when its core processes and services become interchangeable, and what does a componentized business look like? What are the advantages of componentization? In this chapter, we examine these whats, whys, and hows of componentization and identify both the growth opportunities they open up and the problems they create.

Redefining Business Components

Business components are the equivalent of interchangeable manufacturing parts but are instead composed of processes, functions, services, and activities: capabilities. A business component is a set of related capabilities that companies carry out on a daily basis. A company might define "marketing" as a component, but so is "advertising," and within advertising is "copy writing." This scoping decision—handling marketing as a total component versus decomposing it to advertising or breaking it down into more subelements—is determined by its deployment as a *capability* in the firm's value webs rather than its function in internal operations.

In automobile manufacturing, the engine might be considered a component in one instance, whereas in another, it's the spark plug. By outsourcing the manufacturing of the X3, BMW will focus on engine design while outsourced manufacturer Magna Steyr and its value web of parts suppliers will meticulously break down every element to what may be thought of as the atomic level.

Management must decide on the types of componentized capabilities the firm wants to use to build its profitable growth and the roles these capabilities play in its value webs. The practical steps of deciding on the business priorities for componentization are addressed in later chapters. There are three levels of components: composite, bundled, and atomistic.

Composite components are marketing, supply chain management, or human resource administration. They are capabilities that a company accesses as a whole from a value web partner that generally brands them as a service. If the company plans to outsource them, there is no reason to break them down into components; the only need is to make sure that there are standardized interfaces, which may require investment in process improvement and IT platforms.

Bundled components are clusters of processes, such as advertising within marketing, procurement within supply chain management, and new-hire document processing within HR administration.

Atomistic components are the specific activities within processes.

Regardless of the chosen level of definition, business components include the people, systems, and any other resources necessary to accomplish the result that justifies calling it a "capability." Companies create growth, build value, and avoid commoditization *only* by linking these capabilities together within the organization and between organizations in a value web. To be a component, a set of business activities or processes simply must have a *standardized interface* with other components. Without the interface, the business parts are not interchangeable, and you have the lurking danger of proprietary interfaces. That systematization and packaging not easy to achieve; they have occupied the auto industry for more than a decade and dominated the restructuring of the consumer electronics industry.

Standardized interfaces usually mean that no one party controls the use of the interface. Instead, they open up competition by making one firm's processes, products, or services substitutable for another's and therefore inevitably accelerate commoditization, fueled by the pressures for efficiency and cost reduction. Companies that can maintain a proprietary interface thrive—for a while. They make their own parts, control their value chains, set terms for suppliers, generate a premium price, and own their unique designs. Once standardized interfaces move to the forefront, these proprietary firms are pushed into a defensive position and eventually lose their leadership position. To be fair, this proprietary position used to work in the era of value chains, as AT&T's control of who could connect devices to its network showed. Now, anyone can connect just about anything to the public phone system.

Standardized interfaces remove value chain control and open up value web coordination. Credit cards are an example of such interfaces; you can use any provider's card at an ATM, airline self-check-in machine, or over the Web. You can also switch providers routinely and automatically. The billions of dollars of Internet e-commerce would not happen without the credit card as a payment mechanism and the standardized menu for entering your card data.

An Industry Moves to Interchangeable Business Parts

The U.S. mortgage business provides an instructive starting point for discussing the nature and impact of componentization, but we could have picked airline reservations, credit cards, Internet portals, car manufacturing, or retailing instead. The mortgage industry is extremely fragmented[1] with real estate agents, mortgage brokers, mortgage bankers, appraisers, title companies, mortgage insurers, document specialists, county recorders, investors, and, of course, the buyers and sellers on behalf of whom this is all meant to work.

There is no way that such a complex set of interactions could ever be "integrated," "streamlined," or "reengineered," but it is being synchronized in new ways through interchangeable process parts and standardized interfaces. The industry has long been built upon separate organizations performing different roles in the mortgage-creation process. Customers may not even see the banker or mortgage broker with whom they originate the process or the appraiser who visits the property or be fully aware of the credit checks that will be made by a third party. Once their mortgage is approved, customers write a check or authorize an electronic payment to the institution that manages their payment processing that, over the life of the loan, may change any number of times. Customers also have to fill out an application and sign a pile of documents at closing. That is just the tip of the iceberg. Behind the scenes, the mortgage business has long been a muddle of unstandardized definitions, documents, procedures, pricing, timetables, and processes.

There are two giant players, Freddie Mac and Fannie Mae, that are intermediaries in the flow of mortgage loan financing, issuing, securitization, and reselling. Once they implemented procedures based on the XML standard for document and data interchange, these two organizations forced the entire industry to a common interface, setting the stage for a new mortgage industry built on interchangeable business parts. This was not automatic or fast, but it was inevitable. Industry administrative costs were escalating, and margins were under pressure in an era of falling interest rates and rapidly increasing refinancing. Freddie Mac and Fannie Mae supported the voluntary industry trade association, MISMO, which began introducing initiatives in 1999.[2] This resulted in agreements on rationalization and standardization of 3,000 business terms in a data dictionary, agreements on legally binding submission and acceptance of legally binding electronic documents, and the adoption of XML and XHTML (an XML-compatible variant of HTML).

Once Freddie Mac and Fannie Mae implemented the MISMO interfaces, other companies could not afford to ignore the innovation. They needed to do business with the organizations, and once the other large players standardized, the market became componentized. The previous masses of forms and procedures were now communication and processing packages. The industry built capabilities that enabled large and small players to benefit from the electronic component. Freddie Mac's software application, Loan Prospector, became the hub in a hub-and-spoke web and included such new componentized services as online automated underwriting and vendor services (appraisals, flood and title insurance, and so on). Fannie Mae's Desktop Originator[3] provides services for credit unions, mortgage brokers, and other industry groups. It added components for single-family lending and servicing, including investor accounting, secondary marketing, and shipping and delivery.

The same standards are being adopted across the ecosystem. Internet-based leaders, such as Lending Tree, make their money mainly from electronic referral fees of, typically, $450, to 150 lenders while seeking the best deal for their customers. The volume of online mortgages grew from around $20 billion in 2000 to more than $160 billion in 2001, and Washington Mutual alone expected to handle $100 billion in 2004.[4] These are small numbers in comparison to the total market, but even if they grow at the typical e-commerce rate of 20 percent annually, they are already adding to the commoditization of basic mortgage services and processing.

These trends and their results are ones that occur again and again and will force more and more industries into consolidation and restructuring. Mortgages are a $6.3 trillion industry. The mortgage ecosystem restructuring has been massive and transformative, yet there was nothing innovative—no sense of radical new ideas, players, or products. All that happened was that paperwork and processes for handling loan origination were turned into components via standardized interfaces.

In 1994, the top 10 mortgage lenders had a 25 percent market share, and the top 25 had a 40 percent market share. Now, the top 5 have 50 percent of the market, and the top 25 have a 79 percent market share. Componentization facilitates advantages of scale and process rationalization. It removes differentiations in products and services that previously compensated for cost inefficiencies. It also has eliminated the need for intermediaries, such as small brokers who were replaced by an electronic link to one of the giants. New intermediaries will emerge, but they will do so by competing on new capabilities, not old ones.

This summary of one of the largest industries in the economy illustrates a pattern that is similar to the changes in travel agencies and credit cards. In all these instances, the winners win big, and less agile companies and smaller players fall into commodity hell.

Li & Fung: A Growing and Growing Componentized Business

The home mortgage example encompasses an industry. The more immediate innovation opportunity is for a company to exploit the componentization and commoditization link before it is pushed into catch-up or commodity hell.

Li & Fung is a highly profitable, rapidly growing global apparel firm that "detaches critical links in the apparel industry's supply chain and finds the best solution for each step." In other words, its entire business is built on components that it deploys, integrates, and synchronizes on behalf of 7,500 factories—none of which it owns or manages but that add up to a million-employee capability—and 350 customers, mostly leading U.S. and European retailers.

The power of this on demand integration is illustrated by an example from The Limited retail chain. It informed Li & Fung that it needed 100,000 garments. There was a small catch: Styles and colors couldn't be specified until the very last minute. No problem whatsoever for Li & Fung. It coordinated its value web, reserving dyes from one supplier, locking in weaving and cutting capacity from others, and delivering— or rather having someone else deliver—the goods in five weeks, not the typical three months.

As a broker, Li & Fung was increasingly squeezed by the power of large buyers and factories, quite literally caught in the middle. Now, Li & Fung is what writer John Hagel describes as a supply chain "orchestrator."[5] Its response to the business squeeze was to remove itself from the role of direct intermediary, connecting buyers and sellers, and instead coordinate multiple levels and parties. "To produce a garment, the company might purchase yarn from Korea and have it woven and dyed in Taiwan, cut in Bangalore, and then shipped to Thailand for final assembly, where it will be matched with zippers from a Japanese company and, finally, delivered to geographically dispersed retailers in quantities and time frames specified well in advance."[6] The value web is composed of componentized partners, any number of which can be assembled and coordinated to meet a customer's demand.

> *Li & Fung doesn't own* any *of the facilities used in any of the processes and activities.*

It is far from a traditional value chain firm: To build that would require an investment of billions of dollars and a massive organization. Instead, Li & Fung builds size by weaving a services web that spans the globe without having to maintain global points of physical presence. Nonetheless, the company plays an integral coordination role in processes that produce billions in manufacturing and retail revenues and that is indispensable to all parties in the value web.

The structure of Li & Fung reflects its role in its web. As John Hagel goes on to describe, "The company has pursued a leveraged growth strategy. It reorganized the company, moving away from an earlier structure built around geography, to a new structure led by small, customer-centric divisions." It componentized its business.

The new organization enables and encourages "lead entrepreneurs" to focus the business on adding value for the customer. "Rather than trying to build or acquire all the specialized processing and transport facilities required to service these customers, Li & Fung focuses on developing deep understanding of the specialized capabilities of existing businesses operating around the world.... When Li & Fung adds a processing facility to its web, it does not view the relationship as a short-term commercial one. It strives to become an important source of business for that facility over the long term, averaging about 30 to 70 percent of its production.... [it] relies on economic incentives rather than detailed contracts or operating agreements to gain access to a highly diverse array of assets around the world."

Nike also orchestrates value webs in order to add value to its own products, but the difference is that unlike Nike, Cisco, and similar companies, Li & Fung does not make any products of its own. Thus, it can offer its relationship and coordination services to any product manufacturer and vendor without being concerned about conflicts of control. This is not a better approach than Nike's, however, just a different way of producing aggressive growth.

Li & Fung doubled its revenues between 1996 and 2000, and its return on invested capital averaged over 30 percent, a huge figure in this low-margin, low-return industry. This last metric is core to its economic efficiency. The 30 percent return comes from its using so little capital; its fixed assets are under 5 percent of revenues. One of the most distinctive advantages of the component-based firm that operates via on demand relationships is an edge in capital efficiency. Studies of supply chain management and logistics show that the top 10 percent of componentized performers in any industry use half the working capital per unit of revenue when compared to the average for their industry. Supply chain management is the earliest and most sustained move to On Demand Business via componentization of all major business functions. Procurement, manufacturing, distribution, and freight are also now accomplished more and more via multiparty value webs. One industry commentator has suggested that in the consumer electronics field, it's no longer Company A competing with Company B but rather Supply Chain Y competing with Supply Chain Z.

Li & Fung continues to grow. Its revenues increased by 13 percent in 2002, and its net profits grew by 38 percent, whereas inventories dropped a further 10 percent. In 2003, Li & Fung saw increases of 26 percent in revenue and 22 percent in profit.

Li & Fung has woven a value web that spans a larger and larger space, and every player gains from being part of this web. Here are examples of the value-added options that Li & Fung creates for itself, its customers, and its many partners.

- "A single factory is relatively small and doesn't have much buying power; that is, it is too small to demand faster deliveries from *its* suppliers. We come in and look at the entire supply chain." Li & Fung then ensures that the small factory has the resources necessary so that the customer receives the product as promised.

- Li & Fung's centrality in its web means that it can optimize overall costs across the web by *increasing* individual units' costs. Companies operating in the web try to minimize their own costs in handling shipments, which can lead to overall inefficiencies. In a typical manufacturing scenario, ten factories will ship full containers of product to ten distribution centers that send these on to a consolidator. The consolidator then unpacks and repacks them. Li & Fung instead takes on the coordination responsibility and arranges for individual containers to move from one factory to another and then ships direct to the *customer*'s distribution center, bypassing the intermediaries. The individual shipping costs are higher, but the total systems cost is lower.

- "If we don't own factories, how can we say we are in manufacturing? Because, of the fifteen steps in the value manufacturing chain, we probably do ten." "Do" is somewhat misleading in this context, however; Li & Fung's value web partners execute; the company coordinates.

- "As a pure intermediary, our margins were squeezed. But as the number of supply chain options expands, we add value for our customers by using information and relationships to manage the network. We help companies navigate through the world of expanded choice."

- "At one level, Li & Fung is an information node, flipping information between our 350 customers and 7,500 suppliers. We manage that all today with a lot of phone calls and faxes and on-site visits. Soon we will have a sophisticated information system with very open architecture to accommodate different protocols from suppliers and from customers...."[7]

Hong Kong, where Li & Fung is headquartered, has around 300,000 small- and medium-sized companies. Forty percent of these are transnational. Hong Kong operates around 50,000 factories in southern China, employing 5 million workers. "Hong Kong is producing a new breed of company. I don't think there will be many the size of General Motors or AT&T. But there will be lots of focused companies that will break into the *Fortune* 1000."[8]

Figures 3.1 and 3.2 illustrate the dramatic impact of the apparel manufacturing value web. Figure 3.1 diagrams the traditional value chain whereby a manufacturer carries out all the functions contained in the central rectangle, including design, fashion planning, manufacturing operations, warehousing, and billing. As in the standard value chain, to the left are suppliers that provide raw materials via shippers; to the right are retailers that buy the apparel maker's goods.

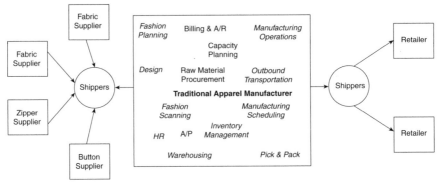

Figure 3.1   The traditional apparel value chain.

The chain is highly disjointed. For instance, the apparel company faces many risks in fashion scanning, planning, and design. It tracks and assesses trends, and although it confers with many experts and customers, it has to make the judgments on what goods to produce in what style and what volume. The retailer similarly has to commit to large orders in advance. This is a difficult formula to get right and explains the high percentage of fashion goods that are disposed of through cheap outlets or bargain tables in stores.

Figure 3.2 captures Li & Fung's componentized value web. Instead of being a chain, with the links wide apart, Li & Fung's operates as a hub; it coordinates rather than controls based on retailers' demands and supplier and manufacturer capabilities and capacities.

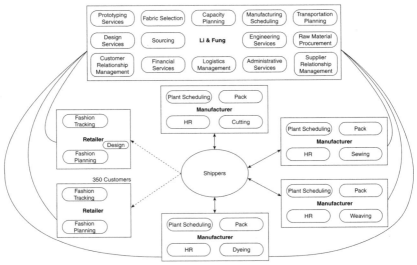

Figure 3.2   Li & Fung's componentized value web.

In the traditional chain, manufacturing, scheduling, and operations occur inside the firm, and scheduling is itself driven by the manufacturer's forecasts of demand. In the value web, manufacturing scheduling is a Li & Fung component applied across many factories, with Li & Fung the overall coordinator. Now, fashion tracking, planning, and design have been pushed out to where they should be: the retailer, which is closest to the end customer. Retailer demand and experience drive manufacturing.

In Chapter 5, "Integrate Your Business Components End-to-End," we explain how a value web expands the firm's growth space by helping other companies innovate with their own componentization, using the platform provided by the web hub operator. We want to emphasize the componentization achieved by Li & Fung; the later TAL example highlights how components can be synchronized to expand the firm's growth space and growth rate.

Componentization is not the rearrangement of building blocks but the basis for configuring the business for growth. In Figure 3.2, the internal operations of Li & Fung are marked by new components, such as customer relationship management, which has become the base for its global organizational structure. Because the coordination and planning functions have been componentized, the old sales force and industry marketing groups are now tightly focused on targeted customer relationships; sales and marketing are now an organizational component that interfaces with the planning components. From the perspective of the planning groups, the factories and suppliers are components with coordination handled through a heavy flow of messages. The shippers are now part of a platform that permits the consolidation of containers and other process innovation.

It all begins with componentization. Without that, the shift from the traditional value chain to value webs cannot be achieved.

Why Componentize?

If your only answer to this question was that you have no choice, this would be a short, depressing book. All that companies could then see on the horizon is outsourced everything, layoffs, price cuts, restructuring charges, and being gobbled up by larger companies.

A few observations suggest otherwise.

- Companies that have sustained growth and profits are consistently in commodity industries with componentized businesses: Wal-Mart in retailing, Dell in computers, and Southwest in airlines.

- Speeches given by their CEOs about General Electric's and eBay's growth strategies are so similar in tone and focus that they are basically interchangeable, and it can be difficult to discern which speaker is which. Their constant themes are standardization and centralization, which sound like the bureaucratic opposite of the innovation that they see enabling their firms.

- Global sourcing has taken on a new scale and moved quickly from low-level manufacturing assembly work to the very core of developed countries' innovation base—its information technology talents, research and development, and design creativity. Does everyone see it as a way simply to cut costs, or are some seeing much more?

- It makes so much sense for BMW, the leader in the high end of the car "manufacturing" market, to contract out the production of its top-of-the-line X3 series sports utility vehicle to a specialist firm, Magna, making it a non-BMW BMW.

Why componentize? It helps grow.

Components with Standardized Interfaces

It is difficult to overstate the impact of standard interfaces in helping move from complexity to simplicity. On an everyday basis via a standard interface, many of us access and use in our business or personal life business services that provide simplicity, even though they are extraordinarily complex. The interface hides the complexity.

- **Shipping**—If you are a small business, FedEx is a service that you can dial up or log on to and forget about it. From your perspective, FedEx is a component in your value web. You need know nothing about how FedEx works, and you never have to phone around or track down people. Your business is stronger because you can access any FedEx business services, such as picking up returned goods or managing your just-in-time inventory. Because FedEx has componentized its business, it can offer a wider array of services and even change its internal processes and systems without affecting you.

  You don't have to know and don't care what goes on inside, because it just works. By contrast, doctors, patients, hospitals, or government health and social services agencies cannot treat the typical health insurer as a component. Little is standardized, and multiple forms, formats, administration, and overhead impede organizational agility. It is a muddle of individual hands-offs and uncoordinated independent activities.

- **Shopping**—Buying a shirt at JC Penney or ordering a pair of custom-made jeans from Lands' End have one surprising element in common: Neither company has anything to do with the product. They take the order, acting purely as the interface. TAL in Hong Kong does forecasting based on point-of-sales data, coordinates the firms whose individual business components—dyeing, cutting, sewing, packing, and shipping—create the final product, and delivers the item of clothing to each store or direct to the customer. JC Penney has cut its warehouse and in-store inventory as a result. The retailers simply treat TAL's services as a component in their own business.

These services are simple to use because they are componentized with clean interfaces. All you do is call, log on, plug in, or pick up. It's easy, consistent, and reliable. As a customer, why accept anything else?

In conclusion, there are three very good reasons to componentize your business: because you have no choice in the long run, because you gain the growth advantage, and because it makes life easier for your customers.

Summary

Businesses are increasingly defined by their ability to produce and integrate with business components. These business components are disparate elements that, when stitched together intelligently, produce industry-leading value webs that redefine the entire market segment. Componentization produces growth opportunities, but it also creates problems and challenges that some firms will not be able to overcome. The simplistic approach to components is outsourcing, but companies don't become market leaders through outsourcing; they do it through building value webs and offering innovative, unique, and high-value components to the web along with coordination capabilities.

4

CREATING BUSINESS COMPONENTS

M ost companies today are not built on components. Instead, they're built as what we call organizational monoliths. A monolith works but at a high cost of communication, rework, duplication, and delay. The tight interdependence of a monolith has a deadly consequence in a commoditized world: When the system is put under pressure, something has to give. And that something is too often service. As the commodity hell gets hotter, the company cannot raise prices or pass on its cost increases. Trapped in a monolithic organization, it also cannot easily reduce its administrative overhead. In a world of commoditization, companies can afford service only through process excellence, a combination of sourcing best-practice components and building internal, reusable best-practice capabilities via components.

The Ford Warranty Approval Process

Five years ago, Ford Motor Company's warranty approval process—the process by which dealers are reimbursed for services performed under warranty—took 60–90 days; now it takes 23 days. It requires the coordination of up to 15 different departments spread throughout four continents, and information has to be accessed or input to 13 transaction-processing systems. The approval process encompasses Ford's major brands: Ford, Lincoln/Mercury, Jaguar, and Volvo. Charles Ragan, Lead Developer for Information Technology and E-Business Infrastructure at Ford Motor Company, describes the warranty approval process as such: "Warranty and recall work is the emergency room of Ford Motor Company.... Losses or savings here can affect the company's financial position and shareholder value."[1]

Standardizing the interfaces between process elements allowed Ford to cut cycle time 60 percent, to 23 days. The *process* itself is still not standardized, and engineers, dealers, and finance and sales personnel continue to work in the same way as before. The difference is that their messages are now coordinated. Instead of the customer service manager responsible for handling a claim having to place phone calls, archive e-mails, and store faxes, all information is routed to a central database, and there is a single software system that coordinates all the data and status reports. As with any major change, there was a cultural challenge, to end workarounds—informal deals whereby people would bypass required procedures and maintain their own private information, without updating "official" data.

Each component is what we call a *commitment unit*. The process has been mapped and broken down into these units, whereby the owner of each unit has the option of accepting or rejecting a request for service. If the owner accepts the request, the owner promises to fulfill and follow through on all aspects of that fulfillment. This structure breaks up the process into components that the system can easily manage. The component interface has three elements: request messages, progress messages, and delivery of the final product. Standardizing the process interface makes it straightforward to coordinate commitments.

Ford is breaking down its monolithic structure in favor of componentization for a 60 percent improvement in cycle time. Ford's interface also normalizes messages so that all information is automatically shared. At Ford, the warranty process has been componentized; now Ford has the *option* of outsourcing some of these components to a service provider, whereas outsourcing was impossible before the componentized system was implemented. Frankly, no one would have wanted it!

An obvious question is how a key process could grow so diffuse and burdensome in a well-run company like Ford. The answer is that this happens everywhere. In monolithic companies, processes are typically handled as administrative overhead. They expand over years—even decades—and add complexity, paperwork, communications, and more. Business-process reengineering tried to streamline such processes but inevitably treated the process as a single component and tried to rationalize its flows and activities. The Ford approach, the Let Go to Grow approach, is to break the process down into its component parts and coordinate them via a standardized interface. In effect, Ford reinvented, not reengineered, these processes.

GE's Componentization Process

Not all components have a marketable value outside the firm; the main impact of creating them will be in building internal agility. The impact of process componentization as a basic organizational discipline is explained by GE CEO Jeff Immelt in his summarization in a late-2003 speech about the decomposition and recomposition of the firm.[2] His talk explains why leading companies are being forced to evolve their growth-platform initiatives, regardless of their industry or specific business model. That evolution begins with the decomposition—the componentization—of the business through simplification, standardization, and outsourcing. In parallel, resources and investments in innovation shift toward the customer relationship, looking to integrate the customer's operations into the company's capabilities. *Innovation* is then increasingly centered on transforming cycle time, responsiveness, and adaptability, which are all vital attributes for a company that can thrive in an on demand world.

The move to an end-to-end platform is driven by componentization and, ironically, increases commoditization at the same time. Immelt echoes our own thoughts when he points out the greatest and most unstoppable forces for commoditization: overcapacity created by technology, manufacturing and supply chain productivity, and global competition. "If you can't differentiate yourself in this world, you get commoditized instantly. We've got to constantly be working on simplification, outsourcing, and process entitlement as ways to make the company better, more efficient, more productive."[3] To accomplish this at GE, business processes are attacked one by one. "We talk a lot in GE about process entitlement. If we do something in five days and the process entitlement is two days, how do we go from five days to two days? And we institute common processes. When we find a process where we think we can improve the entitlement, we drive that across the company. We don't allow that notion that says, "I'm different." In fact, we tell people, 'You're the same.'"[4]

Jeff Immelt is not saying that everything across the business is standardized, because that would destroy the very innovation that he is trying to foster. But *different* and *innovative* are not the same thing. Many different operational processes consume the resources needed for innovation. GE's operational priorities start with reducing complexity everywhere. "We're really looking to our company to have fewer P&Ls, fewer legal entities, fewer suppliers." The next priority is to drive standards toward "common systems architecture, common practices, digitization across that [and] accelerating acquisition integration."[5] The last of the top priorities at GE is going for "as many centralized approaches as we can to drive speed and cost. I think the whole trick is in how you simplify your company to minimize your back room."[6] Immelt is leading GE to allocate more resources to satisfy customers and drive growth.

> *Allocate more resources to satisfy customers and drive growth.*

Immelt concludes, "Our business goal is growth. We wake up every morning trying to focus on that. Driving growth really requires investment and innovation and a total connection with the customer. Funding this growth requires simplification."[7]

One of GE's subsidiaries, GE Healthcare, illustrates how these priorities can fuel new growth. Simplification, rationalization, focus, and centralization enabled the unit to set up centers of excellence—new organizational components—that cut costs and speed up development. These improvements facilitate global expansion through product platform management rather than individual product management, which also increases the opportunity to source lower-cost parts. Between 60 percent and 95 percent of GE Healthcare products are now shipped from the countries of manufacture.

GE is an old-economy company, but its thinking is very close to that of such leading electronic-commerce companies as Amazon and Yahoo!. It is also similar to Dell, Cisco, and Schwab, companies that began operations before the Internet explosion but were quick to exploit the opportunities for interfacing and on demand responsiveness that it opened up. Different companies, different markets, different customers: common business logic.

Innovation does not disappear in a world of components; companies with platforms just change the rules. Sometimes, this is through design skills; sometimes, through supply chain excellence; sometimes, through process transformation; and sometimes, through partnerships. The standardized interfaces remain fixed or change on a common industry basis to ensure standardization. The business capabilities shift, and there is a continual search for new ways to create component-based value.

Componentizing P&G

Procter and Gamble was one of 18 firms identified in *Built to Last*[8] as visionary companies that succeeded through timeless management principles. P&G was praised for its commitment to ensuring well-trained managers at every level of its hierarchy. Other firms have also been the beneficiaries of its talent base and the management development that leveraged it: the CEOs of GE (Jeff Immelt), eBay (Meg Whitman), Microsoft (Steve Ballmer), and AOL Time Warner (Steve Case).

P&G developed operations platforms for integrating every element of its value chain. For decades, it dominated its core markets. It was a powerhouse of individual brands, with very little coordination among them. There was no superordinate P&G brand, and customers were mostly oblivious to the fact that their kitchens, bathrooms, and laundry rooms were full of P&G products. Customers simply knew that they bought Ivory, Pampers, Crisco, or L'Oreal products.

P&G aimed to double its sales every decade, a target that amounts to a 7 percent annual increase. P&G ran out of growth in the mid-1990s. From 1997 to 2001, its sales increased by only 2.4 percent a year.[9] Analysts began to refer to P&G as "venerable"[10] and known for its steady earnings growth and conservative management. Competitive intensity increased as power moved from manufacturers to retailers and as globalization made it more and more difficult to use brand equity as the driver of sales in new markets.

P&G needed to rev up its growth engines.

Alan Lafley, CEO of P&G, endorsed the need for change and is shifting P&G from having a control strategy to a Let Go to Grow strategy. His governance principle is that P&G should focus on what it is best at *and nothing more*, which requires opening up the company and means that this previously secretive and insular firm has to learn to let go. For instance, Lafley has mandated that half of all new products must come from outside the company, whether by acquisition, joint ventures, or collaborations. Already, a reported 20 percent of new-product initiatives are externally generated, twice what P&G was reporting when he took office in late 2000.

Lafley explains, "I'm very externally focused. I expressed the change in the context of how we're going to serve consumers better, how we're going to win with the retailer, and how we're going to defeat the competitor in the marketplace. I preserved the core of the culture and pulled people where I wanted to go. I enrolled them in the change. I didn't tell them."[11] When asked how he paced change, he responded, "I have tremendous trust in my management team. I let them be the brake. I am the accelerator. I help with direction and let them make the business strategic choices." On the subject of shifting the R&D focus externally, he said, "It will be a challenge, but I think we'll get there. It's like a flywheel. That first turn is really difficult. Then the second turn is a little bit easier."[12]

P&G highlights the leadership, management, and cultural aspects of the componentization process. Once vision and the desired rules for change have been established, they must be communicated and the transition managed within the context of the existing culture, even knowing that the culture must also change. Push too hard, and the people push back. Don't push hard enough, and nothing changes.

P&G has now let go of manufacturing and opened up its intellectual property portfolio. For example, in 2002, P&G licensed all its current and future patents, trademarks, and proprietary technologies to competitor Clorox, for its Glad line of products. P&G gets a 10 percent stake in Clorox's sales, plus royalties. In 1998, Paragon Trade Brands filed for bankruptcy shortly after a judgment against them for infringing on a P&G patent.[13] Today, P&G licenses all 28,000 of its patents.

P&G has been a leader in information technology for decades, including helping pioneer Collaborative Planning, Forecasting, and Replenishment (CPFR). Starting in the 1980s, CPFR enabled P&G to manage its own inventory on Wal-Mart shelves via electronic linkages between the store point-of-sale systems and P&G's systems. P&G outsourced its entire 2,000-employee IT function to Hewlett-Packard, transferring the staff. P&G has also been a leader in manufacturing operations and now outsources all bar-soap manufacturing, including Ivory, its oldest brand. P&G has taken further steps as it has Let Go to Grow by dismantling corporate administrative functions, sourcing its human resource administration to IBM Global Services.

Lafley commented, "My hypothesis is that innovation and discovery are more likely to come from anywhere. What P&G is really good at is developing innovations and commercializing them. So what I said is, 'We need an open marketplace. Our core capability is to develop and commercialize. Branding is a core capability. Customer business development is a core capability. Manufacturing isn't. Therefore, I let the businesses do more outsourcing.'"[14] Lafley ended with the key point that highlights the company's transition from control to Let Go to Grow: "You do what you do best and can do world-class." Everything else you get from outside, from your value web partners.

P&G is not just outsourcing, *it is building core capabilities*. It is expanding its beauty care brands with the purchase of Clairol and Wella and leveraging its brand and distribution capabilities by expanding its value web to include over-the-counter healthcare products, such as Prilosec. To effect this sweeping change, A. G. Lafley established and communicated a vision. He clearly stated the governance rules and insisted that they focus only on what P&G does best and nothing more. P&G is outsourcing everything else and building capabilities through value web expansion.

When they open themselves up to outside relationships, companies like P&G typically start by trying to use standard outsourcing. P&G initially planned to outsource HR administration on a contract basis, for example, but soon realized that it must first componentize its own processes to ensure clean interfaces that allowed links between P&G and its service provider. We refer to this as *cosourcing* rather than outsourcing: creating a relationship rather than merely a transaction.

Componentizing the Business

The starting point for componentization is often administrative processes and the standard operations of the firm. Standardization via interfaces, as we just observed with Ford, GE, and P&G, will undoubtedly benefit your firm. But it can't stop there. Letting Go to Grow is all about building capabilities, not simply outsourcing. There are four main choices for mapping components and prioritizing their value web contribution.

1. Achieve competitive superiority through components that are specific to the firm and are competitive differentiators; design and marketing are often-cited examples.

2. Leverage process specialists to create generic but still profitable differentiators; use value web relationships to mirror the structure of Li & Fung.

3. For those activities that are specific to the firm and non-differentiating, adopt the GE approach of standardization, centralization, and reuse. Common examples are scheduling, financial accounting, and international coordination.

4. Finally, for those many processes and commodity operations that add no differentiation and are generic, outsource them as components from the appropriate providers.

An *interface* can be summarized as "let's connect." The key design challenge is to define the interface point, interface mechanism, and interface message standard. All three are required and constitute a standardized interface. Whether it is an engine connecting to a transmission, a planning system connecting to a purchasing system, or a customer connecting to a service center, the principle is the same. A standardized interface means, "We can connect without either of us having to change what we do and how we do it." A proprietary interface amounts to "Sure, let's connect—but only if *you* change your product or systems and meet *our* requirements." The lack of a clearly defined interface or the proliferation of multiple interfaces results in "Sorry, it won't work."

The term "standardization" immediately suggests a single way of handling something or a single product design. It's Henry Ford's famous statement that customers could have any color Model T as long as it was black. "Standard operating procedure" typically means "bureaucracy," and "nonstandard" suggests an exception, a nuisance, and an increase in cost.

Standardization of *interfaces* actually maximizes the variety of design options for the components themselves. One example is the wide range of features of digital cameras that all share the same hardware interface options, photo and video standards (JPEG, MPEG, and so on), and links to PCs and printers. The creativity goes into designs, and products differentiate through speed and quality, but each new camera maintains the same interfaces. As new interfaces become standardized, new devices exploit them.

In the world of proprietary interfaces, by contrast, products created standards, as the competition between VHS and Betamax illustrates. In the world of business components, however, it's the opposite: Standards create products. The mortgage industry's adoption of standardized interfaces for electronic transactions and document handling has opened up a wide variety of new process-based services that Fannie Mae, Freddie Mac, Lending Tree, and others can now offer to partners and clients alike.

For business service, value web coordination, and collaboration, none of this is as easy. When BMW outsourced the entire manufacturing of its X3 series, turning manufacturing into a business component, the interface was considerably more complex than simply plugging in a cable: The contract alone was 5,000 pages long! The principle of innovation on your side of the interface applies here, just as it does for digital cameras and mortgage services. Magna, which is manufacturing the X3, is encouraged to innovate on the manufacturing components, as long as it remains in compliance with the interface.

Moving to Standardized Electronic Interfaces

Li & Fung is basically an interface among multiple parties. The new information system it is building, with its open architecture to accommodate different protocols from suppliers and customers, creates new interface capabilities that help increase on demand synchronization. To achieve this goal, Li & Fung first standardized the form and content of the information passed between companies and then built its growth through fax, mail, and phone call interfaces, which are primitive but still vital in the emerging era of standardized products, processes, services, and technologies. The collaborative trust that is one of Li & Fung's main cultural assets and capabilities is also the reason why small suppliers commit to meeting its specified dates for production. Capabilities built from components plus standardized interfaces plus collaborative relationships create a powerful platform for even more growth.

Standard interfaces are a historic inevitability, driven by customer choice in every business ecosystem. USB, for example, is simply a physical symbol for a movement that encompasses not only product components but also *any* process or business function that can be componentized and turned into a capability that has a well-defined interface and measurable market value.

"Plastics." That was the career advice that Dustin Hoffman received in the 1967 film *The Graduate*. Today, almost 40 years later, we'd say "standardized interfaces" as a career direction. It is the standardization of interfaces that is driving the componentization of individual companies and entire industries. Whether GE or Amazon, componentization has become the foundation of effective Let Go to Grow companies. Whether it's an old-economy GE or an Internet-firm Amazon, componentization of business is the operational core.

Getting Components Right

Creating components requires a related set of activities and processes, along with the associated people skills and systems. This is what we call a Bound, Bind, and Bundle approach to business operations and innovation:

- **Bound**—Identify the activities and processes that constitute the core of your business, and turn them into well-bounded and systematic components with a clear interface point.

- **Bind**—Link components—your own and those of other players in your value web—via the standardized interfaces that are part of your own platforms.

- **Bundle**—Expand your options by synchronizing components, allowing you to build new capabilities and deliver new or enhanced services to customers.

Bounding Components

How large should a component be? That depends on how it will be used. If you plan to cosource all your manufacturing, manufacturing itself can be the component. If you plan to keep part of it, you will want to slice the process into many more pieces. For example, many companies outsource human resource benefits administration but keep benefits planning in-house.

The fundamental question is, How will a component be used? Will you deploy it internally, leverage it as part of a closely managed relationship, make it available to the open market, or make it available for others to use as part of their own innovation? If the intention is to leverage the component across your own organization, at what level is this most useful, and how will it interface with your other business components? If the intention is to use it as part of a closely held service relationship, at what level will it be of most value to those partners? If you want to sell it on the open market, how do you maximize its external worth? If you decide to source it, how big and complex a component can someone else take?

There are no canned answers to these questions. How to figure out your answer will become more clear when we discuss pivot points in Chapter 5, "Integrate Your Business Components End-to-End." We'll also explain how companies can maximize their growth opportunities through *pivot points*. Pivot points are where growth comes from: your capabilities, customer growth, value web growth, or the ecosystem innovation you help enable. None of these options is available if a process or a function is not bounded as a component or if it cannot be sourced or shared through a standardized interface.

Binding Components

Everything does not have to interface to everything else. The automobile engine has no need to interface with the door handle but does have to interface to the transmission. Accounts payable does not have to interface with leadership development but does have to interface with invoicing and any internal component needed to authorize payment. In the information component world, the technical interface should be standardized, leaving the content to be component specific.

Separating content from interface is exactly what Li & Fung is all about. This is also what Amazon does when it leverages its partners' shipping components to deliver goods, track shipments, and offer free shipping. Amazon accomplishes this through leveraging the capabilities of FedEx and UPS. Such synchronization establishes the variety and scope of the organizational capabilities you can build through bound-then-bind.

Bundling Components

Auto manufacturing and knowledge-intensive industries, such as pharmaceuticals, high tech—the hardware side of which has become very much a commodity market—and financial services, are established industries experiencing a business ecosystem decomposition. They're evolving from "do-as-much-as-we-can-ourselves" organizations to component sourcing, reuse, linkage through value webs, and most of all *options*: in cost structure, investment, capital deployment, and scaling. It all starts with interfaces.

Shipping Isn't a Chore

To grow, a company must be able to configure components on demand and via relationships with third parties. The very same process can be viewed two entirely different ways, highlighting the essence of business componentization. It is the deceptively simple task of handling product shipments purchased online. Shipping is a business capability for Amazon, a company that serves as an exemplar of *Let Go To Grow* through its componentization and On Demand Business and relationships. For many other Internet retailers, however, shipping remains an overhead function. For the *customer*, prompt and reliable shipping is far from overhead and, in many respects, is seen as part of the company's branding. Amazon stands out because of its shipping strategy—free delivery for purchases over a certain minimum amount.

Some of the credit for Amazon's performance belongs to FedEx and UPS, two forward-thinking companies that have created an entire business around third-party logistics, including warehousing, payment collection, and inventory management. FedEx and UPS provide Amazon with a critical component of its business: an impeccable shipping department. Amazon technology and process platforms are tightly coupled to these outsourced solution providers. FedEx and UPS have invested hundreds of millions of dollars in these value-generating assets; Amazon then utilizes those assets on a pay-as-you-go variable-cost basis, with no capital investment in fleets, facilities, or personnel.

By contrast, many other leading online retailers have not structured their shipping as an on-time, cost-effective business component—it was only shipping. Early dot-com pioneer eToys went bankrupt, largely because of unreliable shipping and late delivery of Christmas goods.

It proved to be fatal to promise delivery of a hot new toy by Christmas and have it actually arrive in early January; eToys had poorly bounded shipping and delivery and a poor interface with the core components of marketing and selling. No one knew exactly what was happening in the warehouse, so the firm kept promoting its best-selling products without realizing that they were already out of stock. Processes, systems, and departments carried out their operations largely in isolation, with fragmented linkages and poor interfaces. This interface weakness is a typical situation in even the best-performing companies, largely because of historical organizational structures, modes of operation, and technology constraints on coordination and integration.

It is not enough to simply improve interdepartment interfaces, long the target of business-process reengineering and technology and work-design investments. These changes, if they work at all, merely streamline processes and help improve efficiency and costs. The problem is that they do not leverage *value;* eToys was never able to make shipping and delivery a component of its value web. By contrast, Amazon is now in a position where it can combine its own components with members of its value web via its interfaces: operations to FedEx and UPS, specialists in more and more areas of logistics; to individual technology entrepreneurs, who use its Web Services toolkits to generate innovative products, services, and tools; to Web associations and individuals who act as brokers for Amazon by highlighting books on their own sites and linking buyers to Amazon in return for a commission. Interfacing is Amazon's basic way of doing business.

The Other Half of the Story

What makes the Amazon story possible is not only its own structure and vision but also the Bound, Bind, and Bundle work that FedEx and UPS have done with their own businesses. That enables the two firms to deliver a wide range of logistics services to all their value web partners.

When a customer returns an HP printer for repair, Hewlett-Packard never sees it. UPS's third-party logistics organization picks it up, services it, and returns it. UPS also now manages the replacement-parts inventory for IBM, Compaq (before it was acquired by HP), and Dell through a nationwide complex of warehouses and end-to-end logistics, ensuring that a technician can get needed parts within four hours. For Gateway, UPS offers payment collection. For Fender guitars, UPS handles the critical task of tuning the instrument—in Holland—saving eight days and cutting costs by 4 percent.

When UPS or FedEx leads, other companies are sure to follow. Both companies operate tightly synchronized platforms. They add capabilities that only a platform owner could provide; they are everyday innovators. FedEx now handles pickup of returned goods for retailers, for instance. It turned its legendary tracking systems into a customer self-management component, lowering costs and adding customer service. The internal administrative function became a packaged component that was implemented as a Web Service. In conjunction, these services extended FedEx's customer relationship management and customers' logistics capabilities. When it acquired Kinko's in early 2004, FedEx bought not only a profitable office services firm but also a new set of components that can be added to its logistics value web: storage for customers' spare parts and product inventories. Kinko's adds additional customer warehouses that FedEx utilizes to deliver yet more products to its customers.

The Componentization of the Pharmaceutical Industry

The gap between top-level function and bottom-level process inexorably leads to competitive erosion, sometimes for an entire industry. Organizational monoliths are driven by power, scale, and market dominance. Componentized companies are driven by agility; they obtain scale through relationships. Monoliths are internally focused; componentized firms, externally focused. Monoliths are built to last, not to grow.

The pharmaceutical industry has historically been dominated by large companies that exploit their operating margins, patents, and economies of scale to create competitive machines. This business model began to break down in the late 1990s. The era of monolithic pharma was over by the end of the century. The response of the biggest firms, however, was consolidation through mergers and acquisitions: to expand.

In the past few years, these pharmaceuticals have increasingly invested more financial capital on research and development. They have also spent money on sales and marketing. According to *The Economist*, the number of sales reps employed by U.S. pharmaceutical firms has increased 50 percent in the past four years.[15] Although the average overhead for large U.S. companies is 17 percent of revenues, it is twice as much—almost one-third of revenues—for Big Pharma.

The pharmaceutical industry is being forced to standardize, modularize, and decompose, particularly in research and development, a value component. R&D is treated as the value of the corporation and thus to be protected. The Let Go to Grow firm asks two key questions: Of value to *whom*? and Where and how can we create *extra* value?

A number of the Big Pharma companies are "letting go." Eli Lilly tripled its 7,500 R&D staff through on demand contract research by creating its online InnoCentive scientific forum.[16] In the 1990s, the company had increased its spending on R&D by an average of 14 percent annually but without an increase in new products. Now, it posts thorny chemical problems on InnoCentive, where 6,000 registered scientists in 125 countries are paid up to $100,000 for their time and effort *only if they solve the problem*. From New Jersey to Russia, scientists who have helped Lilly solve specific problems have received a total of $420,000. Lilly posts 80–100 problems a week and sees a 4 percent solution rate, which is very high for R&D. Both Procter & Gamble and Dow Chemical are also using InnoCentive to reduce their own R&D costs. Eli Lilly is turning InnoCentive into a web portal company, a component in many companies' value webs.

A few years ago, Lilly posted an offer to anyone who could help it reduce the manufacturing costs of a chemical compound used in polyester and carpet products. The solution came in minutes from a North Carolina patent lawyer who had worked in an Ohio chemical plant and remembered a comparable problem and its resolution.

Other firms, such as Pfizer, are beginning to view their intellectual capital and research as a business component that offers value opportunities beyond their own product lines. Companies are reaching out to the fast-growing, talent-rich economy of India for pharmaceutical research and development.

Componentization of R&D is helping the pharmaceutical monoliths reinvent themselves. Novartis opened up a new R&D center in Cambridge, Massachusetts, explicitly to improve its relationships with academic researchers. GlaxoSmithKline has split its R&D into smaller centers of excellence and enlarged the unit that leverages their work. Wyeth has componentized its in-house R&D facility.

Previously, early-stage research teams threw their work "over the wall" to the scientists who handled clinical trials before it was ready; such teams were in the business of invention, not implementation. Now, all teams share in the rewards for moving a product from concept to market. Componentization permits specialized differentiation, early-stage skills and processes, and integration, ensuring that differentiated components work together. Differentiation plus integration is componentization in action.

Conclusion: The Executive Agenda

Our first management principle is thus: *Componentize your business.* This is the foundation and key first step in Letting Go to Grow. Your componentized business can create the type of value web that Li & Fung created, simultaneously addressing the value generators of customer demand, retailer delivery, manufacturer production, and intermediary producers. You can emulate a Wal-Mart by eliminating the artificial distinction between customer relationship management and supply chain, integrating all your value components from demand to supply and the reverse. If you don't have a componentized business, you cannot do any of these. Componentization is fundamentally about taking the journey from function to process excellence, to standardization, and to finally arrive at the opportunity to deconstruct and reconstruct your business with components that maximize your value-generating options.

Componentization is also the springboard for *accelerated growth*. Incremental growth is the best you can hope for within a traditional structure where you can expand internal R&D, speed up time to market, or streamline processes. Good companies continually fine-tune their businesses, but dramatic improvements in growth and sustained expansion come only from componentizing. This generates added capabilities and expands the firm's growth space. Firms try to grow by buying new components, that is, mergers and acquisitions, but these produce expansive growth only through componentization: the differentiation that adds new potential value and the integration that realizes the value.

Accelerated growth comes from integrating components—yours and others'—in ways that help your value web differentiate from the competition in real time and in response to market changes.

Swiss Re, the second-largest global reinsurer, has made componentization of acquisitions core to its strategy because, when well managed, competition via standardization can add to invention and creativity, not block it. Several years ago, Swiss Re saw the opportunity to expand by acquiring both blocks of business and financial business units from companies that were leaving the life insurance market. It had substantial expertise in mergers and acquisitions, but the problem it faced with rapid growth through M&A is one that most firms have been unable to solve: smoothly integrating the acquired companies' operations into its own without information systems investments and large-scale reorganizations.

Swiss Re began its expansion in 1995 with 50,000 policies in its portfolio. Within a year, it had 1.4 million policies and was adding 20,000–30,000 a month.[17] Its teams were working on incorporating four new "blocks" of business totaling more than 800,000 policies, run on seven different legacy systems and reflecting seven different processes. The chairman of Swiss Re explained his logic in creating a new value web via cosourcing of technology and processes: "As an insurer, we're a wholesaler. We did not want to hire lots of people to administer policies, build an infrastructure, or upgrade technology so we outsourced that part of the business. Initially, we could provide capital to our clients, but we weren't able to take over administration. Now we can."[18] Clients—the companies whose blocks of business software Swiss Re has acquired—link to Swiss Re via its on demand service.

This componentized value web relationship has given Swiss Re flexibility, speed, scale, and quality. Well over half of mergers, acquisitions, and partnerships fail. The deal is sound and the strategic logic clear, but efforts to integrate processes, systems, and organizations take more time, cost, and effort than expected.

Swiss Re anticipated and resolved this problem in advance. How many companies could scale as quickly and effectively while still keeping everything in-house and trying to integrate existing systems? Componentization gave Swiss Re an in-house capability through a tight relationship with an outside value web partner. As CEO Jacques Dubois commented that for its "client" companies, this is part of Swiss Re itself: "Clients see it as one-stop shopping because they only have to deal with *us*."[19]

Our strong recommendation is to make business transformations through componentization your first priority. This is very different from making business process change or outsourcing a priority. To ensure well-bounded components with strong differentiation and well-defined interfaces for integration, your firm will need to clean up a number of processes first. Equally, the logic of value components as the base for business configuration almost surely means that your company will outsource many functions that it previously kept in-house. But outsourcing is not the value goal, though it may be the cost goal, because cost cutting is not a vehicle for growth. It is the value web enabled by all forms of sourcing that creates the growth opportunity. It's how your firm can Let Go and Grow.

Summary

Agility is becoming a critical factor in market success because it allows companies to react quickly to changes in their market segments and to tailor and customize their offerings to match the changing needs of their customers. That's the core argument for componentization: the reinvention of your company as a set of integrated, interconnected components that allow you to always answer the question: *Is this business configuration optimal?* From Ford to General Electric, Procter & Gamble to Li & Fung, componentized companies are better able to move into the future and create profitable growth than are competitors that retain traditional, monolithic structures.

5

INTEGRATE YOUR BUSINESS COMPONENTS END-TO-END

How does a company ensure that its business components fit together, enabling it to differentiate itself and grow? If it is able to keep up only in the face of competitive intensity, the company inevitably faces a commoditized future and must continuously restructure. In the end, it will not grow profitably over time and will end up just another statistic. The solution is to build a business platform that enables speed, flexibility, adaptability, coordination, collaboration, everyday innovation, and cost optionality. It is only through these capabilities that differentiation is built in a commodity world.

From Components to Platform

To begin, we'll again define *platform*, as the term has so many meanings. A platform is analogous to the launch pad for the space shuttle. It is also a firm and reliable structure foundation, like an oil-drilling platform. Most of all, it is something to build upon. *A platform is a set of business capabilities upon which other capabilities are built, linked, and expanded.*

Components are individual, self-contained capabilities; a platform adds *integration* capabilities to the individual components. It enables a firm to access and coordinate not only its own components but also components across its value web. A platform integrates and facilitates reuse of internal components and enables the company to outsource components, such as centers, yet achieve quality and timely response in addition to cost reduction. This turns outsourcing—getting rid of something—into cosourcing—giving a capability. As with Li & Fung, a good platform enables an organization to create new capabilities without heavy added capital investment and risk. Both Amazon and eBay have a foundation for new sources of revenue through the sale of components, not only products and services.

Creating a platform starts with business vision and governance because it must be designed to support the business direction and desired value web roles and be able to grow in reach, range, and robustness to meet growth needs for scaling. In short, a robust business platform requires much more than merely capabilities. It demands planning and governance, policies, rules, and funding. It also requires rules to address the necessary interface standards, including technology standards, industry practices, and process interfaces, as discussed in the previous chapter.

A bank may decide that its technology blueprint needs to support retailers' interface standards for supply chain management; that decision directly impacts the value web it builds in the retailing space. A retailer may decide to limit its use of financial service standards for transaction processing and payments, on the other hand, to avoid the complexity of handling a growing variety of service options and financial instruments. There is no "right" choice here, but creating a growth platform involves making certain strategic choices and implementing them in as modular a fashion as possible.

> *A platform is a set of business capabilities upon which other capabilities are built, linked, and expanded.*

Cemex: From Domestic Player to Global Pacesetter via Platform

One of the most striking, explicit, and successful exploitations of the platform opportunity is Cemex, the Mexican-based cement maker that moved from number 35 to number 3 in the world within its highly competitive sector. Cemex has led its industry in growth and profits for a decade, despite a number of major handicaps, especially the cost of capital: Being located in Mexico means that the cost of capital is in the high double-digit range versus midrange single digits for North American and European competitors. Cemex's global diversification and performance have cut its cost to around 8 percent, but this still puts the company at a disadvantage compared to its main rivals.

Nonetheless, Cemex's operating margins are twice those of the two larger global players. In the recessionary period of 2001, it grew its sales 25 percent. Between 1985 and 1995, it cut its labor force by 50 percent, to 7,500 employees, while increasing its production capability by 20 percent. From 1990 to 2001, its labor costs increased at a rate of only 4 percent a year, whereas its sales increased 16 percent. When it acquired the two largest Spanish cement makers in 1992—a move that almost all financial analysts saw as a major blunder—it increased their operating margins by 20 percent within two years and by 2000, eight years after the purchase of the subsidiaries, had increased them by a factor of four.[1]

Cemex now operates in more than 30 countries. Over a 15-year period, its revenues grew on average by 21 percent a year, a return on equity by 15 percent per annum, and a return on invested capital of 10 percent. It generates a billion dollars a year of free cash flow against sales of more than $7 billion.

Cemex competes in a highly commoditized industry. Cement is a basic product, and its price is highly cyclical; price and demand closely match economic growth. The business is highly capital intensive, making it very sensitive to economic shifts that boost or bust construction markets. In 1990, the top five firms' total manufacturing capacity was

144 million tons, about 11 percent of global production. By 2001, top-five capacity had grown to 566 million tons, almost 40 percent of global capacity. The financial crisis in Asia in the late 1990s left many half-finished skyscrapers and rusting cranes covering the horizon. Then explosive Chinese economic growth in the early 2000s generated both short-term global shortages and rapid expansion of China's own cement industry.

Cement is a highly localized market because of transportation. The maximum cost-effective shipping distance by land is only 250 miles. Transportation by sea is more profitable, but a country like Thailand can produce cement for around $12 per metric ton and ship it to the U.S. for $30 per ton. Foreign cement manufacturers make money when there are local shortages and lose money when shipment costs increase. A major Cemex innovation in this regard was to use its global satellite network to manage the movement of cement carried on its fleet of ships, sometimes trading the cargo midocean to always direct it to the most profitable market.

At around one ton per person on the planet, cement is second only to water in terms of human consumption. Cement is also controversial in terms of environmental policy, yet Cemex has won many wildlife protection awards—cement plants are big and in remote locations, which can make them a sanctuary if management sets that as a priority. Cemex's leaders have done so for a decade, owing partly to social responsibility and also because it makes business sense. Clean plants and eco-friendly manufacturing leads to lower costs and better relationships with the local inhabitants and encourages investment in improved manufacturing methods.

Cemex is frequently lauded as both the best-run company in Latin America and the most innovative. The most widely reported of these innovations is its wireless links to 1,500 trucks that are dynamically routed to customers' construction sites. Cemex now meets its intensely time-sensitive delivery orders in 20 minutes, versus the previous 3-hour time window, with a delivery-cost reduction of 55 percent and a surge in customer satisfaction. Other Cemex process innovations include the following.

- Its industry-leading Post Merger Integration (PMI) teams move into a new acquisition and integrate all core processes into the "Cemex Way" in under four months.

- Cemex's use of satellite technology and Lotus Notes creates the real-time global executive information system that CEO Lorenzo Zambrano can use to monitor operational performance, down to the level of a factory kiln, even midflight on the corporate jet.

- The creation of Patriemento Hoy—"get your savings today"—allows poor families to save as a group so that each member gets a chance to fund the construction of a home; 15,000 households were signed up by the end of the first year. (The lack of consumer credit in Mexico means that most families have to literally build their homes as they can afford to do so.)

- Mexican workers in the United States can visit a Cemex office and pick out home-building supplies for their families back home. Most of the billions of dollars Cemex workers send back to Mexico are built on their ambition of owning a house. By paying for the building materials on the spot, they avoid the typical 12 percent fee for transferring funds to Mexico.

Cemex's growth was not the result of operating in a beneficial environment. The company has dealt with the peso devaluation of 1995, was hit by an antidumping penalty imposed by the U.S. government, and has had limited price flexibility in its domestic market because the Mexican government sets cement prices.

The Department of Labor reports that the productivity of U.S. manufacturing grew at the fastest rate in 40 years between 1996 and 2003, at 4.6 percent a year.[2] Cemex's growth is two to three times this in the same time period. In particular, Cemex has had a much higher gain in productivity than the U.S. cement industry. In fact, the U.S. industry grew just 0.8 percent a year in that period, the least growth of any major manufacturing industry.

Cemex's growth can be explained only in terms of its management. It is in a nongrowth industry that is barely more productive than it was a decade ago, faces continual financial constraints in capital markets, is in a developing—not developed—economy, and continually faces domestic and international political obstacles largely outside its control.

Componentization and platform were the very foundation of this success. The basic growth drivers in Cemex have been the personality and skill of its CEO, Lorenzo Zambrano; the equal brilliance of its Chief Financial Officer, Gustavo Caballero; the adroitness of its CIO, Gelacio Iniguez; and the componentization, IT, and productivity metrics that comprise the "Cemex Way."

Here are some comments from Zambrano and outside commentators about the Cemex Way componentized platform.

- "The only threat to the realization of Cemex's true potential is the traditional view that the cement industry is static and its products are commodities."[3]

- "We have learned how to identify and share best practices across a global network, in part by installing common business practices and a common information technology platform throughout our system."[4]

- "What we did over the past ten years, I believe we can do even better during the next ten years, in part because of the platform we have built and in part because of the lessons we have learned."[5]

The goal was not standardization for its own sake, but rather a common platform that would enable common performance measures and the development of a common base of business knowledge.

Each Cemex Way team was sponsored by an Executive VP for that core process, and their mandate was to identify the company's best practices, incorporate them into standard platforms, and to then execute them throughout the organization worldwide. Cemex expected the end result to be a cultural shift toward accepting information process standardization.

The Cemex Way is the formalization of a series of componentization and technology initiatives that evolved as Cemex grew from a small domestic company to global giant. Its first acquisition of another Mexican cement maker, Tolteca, spawned two very different cultures for several years, with very different processes and totally different information systems. This pattern continued with the Spanish acquisitions, many of whose employees were unhappy about their new Mexican owner.

Cemex's strategy for growth by acquisition is to buy poorly managed firms—often owned partly by the national government—when they were underfunded, underpriced, and underperforming. The countries that it bought into included Venezuela, India, the United States (a productivity laggard, as the Department of Labor figures demonstrate), Panama, Indonesia, Japan, Thailand, Egypt, Colombia, Chile, and France.

CIO Gelacio Iniguez faced significant challenges bringing the company into the 21st century: Cemex had almost no technology when he joined the firm in the late 1980s. The various operations were very independent, and it was difficult to share information and leverage capabilities. Iniguez saw process standardization and collective technology as the key to Cemex's becoming a growth firm. Over time, with the support of key executives (and substantial opposition from others), Cemex moved in the same direction as GE and eBay, toward standardization of processes, centralization of technology, and, what may well be the single major operational factor in Cemex's international success, its Post Merger Integration team. Indeed, four months to bring an acquisition to Cemex best practice is exemplary for any industry.

Lorenzo Zambrano is a navigator. He is always looking ahead, spotting the next turn of the river and the rapids and rocks ahead. He is obsessed with efficiency. While you're reading this page, Zambrano may be checking on why a plant in Colombia was below its daily production quota. In Chapter 9, "Achieving Measurable Productivity Improvements," we address the issue of enterprise productivity and point to the widespread conflict in many firms between growth and efficiency. The Cemex Way enables, encourages, and rewards both. Cemex is obsessively focused on cost savings, daily results, and the components of operations that are required for delivering these results. It is also obsessively committed to growth—via its platform.

The Cemex Way is built on nine components, including procurement, finance, and operations. The PMI teams are the firm's elite junior managers. They don't impose standardization but look first for frustrated innovators and smart employees who have been blocked by the previous management. Underperformance, the basis for Cemex to acquire a firm, means that there are many such people. The PMI team transfers innovation between Cemex and the acquisition.

The Platform Battle: Toyota Versus the Rest

Toyota builds more cars for less money than does any other automobile manufacturer, by using a set of chassis and frame parts to create a common vehicle architecture: a platform. The vehicle platform is much more than a set of chassis and frame parts, however, and is the direct result of a governance blueprint. Toyota has been assiduous in its planning and implementation.

U.S. carmakers, Toyota's Japanese competitors, and European companies all recognize the need to go beyond component commoditization. All are trying to match the Toyota platform blueprints.

All the top automakers are moving quickly. Innovation is everywhere. There are now two main competitive drivers—design and manufacturing—among the global auto leaders, and U.S. firms are focusing on design while racing to catch up in manufacturing. *Fortune* reported in early 2004 that the Big Three were introducing 48 models that year. Says Daimler Chrysler CEO Dieter Zetsche, "We're going to continue to launch new and exciting vehicles at a fast pace, and attack virtually every segment of the auto market."[6]

But Toyota is not standing still in the face of this reignited competitive spirit.

"Toyota is integrating its assembly plants across the world into a single giant organism that will enable the company to save time—and money—on every car it makes."[7] If that were all that Toyota achieved, however, the platform would offer efficiency but not growth. *Fortune* continues: "This manufacturing network will make it much cheaper to build a wide variety of models. That means that Toyota will be able to fill market niches *as they emerge* without having to build whole new assembly operations. With consumers increasingly fickle about what they want in a car, such market agility gives Toyota a huge competitive edge."[8]

> ## *On demand customers force On Demand Business.*

Any organizational capability is a mix of physical elements, such as a store, warehouse, factory, or employees, and intangible assets, such as information systems, process designs, and intellectual capital. Toyota's "global body line" permits it to adjust this combination at will. *Global* body line is emphasized because Toyota's vehicle platform is a manifestation of its all-encompassing *business* platform. In low-cost labor markets, such as Vietnam, it adds people; and in high-cost markets such as the United States, it adds robots. It gains capital efficiency; the new line requires half the investment needed for the one it replaces and reduces the cost of a new car model by 70 percent.

Toyota has long made processes and relationship management integral to its business platform. It made the collaboration of its supply network the core of its production system by working so closely with its key suppliers that it took charge of their facilities redesign, methods, and TQM processes to ensure the cycle time and quality Toyota required. It provided its tier 1 partners with training and consultation.

The global body line adds both tangible and intangible capabilities. It replaces an older integrated but noncomponentized predecessor, the flexible body line. The flexible body line used three huge pieces of costly precision tooling, known as pallets, to handle the requirements for each product moving along the assembly line. A full line thus required 50 pallets and took up a football field of storage. With the global body line, a single pallet now handles all models. The assembly line requires half as much space and half the process work along the line.

This is powerful in itself, but the competitive edge is honed by Toyota's links between design and manufacturing. The governance rules that ensure this integration are explicit: "Toyota won't design a vehicle that it can't build efficiently."

Design platforms are becoming a major competitive differentiator, and ignoring the importance of design is a source of competitive erosion. The winners will be the companies whose platforms support design through manufacturing.

The important message here is the degree to which a platform can create a massive *structural* competitive differentiator and to suggest that whatever industry your firm is in, it must never get preempted in the way that Cemex and Toyota have pushed its rivals onto the defensive.

From Platform to Value Webs

Componentization is the basis of a growth platform but is not the platform. Componentization creates the opportunity to buy, sell, or leverage business functions as a set of interchangeable parts. Stopping at this step in business evolution leads to commoditization in a negative sense; the company is stuck with all the problems of competing on me-too products, price cutting, and cost cutting everywhere and seemingly forever.

> *Creating new and enhanced business capabilities through component integration is the management challenge and opportunity.*

Integrating them internally enhances your new value proposition. But linking your own firm's capabilities to those of your customers and other companies creates opportunities far beyond those of a traditional value chain. It opens up multiple paths to building *value webs*, whereby a firm can buy and sell components with an unlimited number of companies, on demand, creating new business capabilities.

Important differences between a value chain and a value web center on who is in control and the nature of relationships with outside parties. A value chain is owned by one company. It controls coordination, defines the contractual terms of relationships, and adds suppliers and other sales channels as needed. A value chain is linear and fixed, its purpose to profitably deliver products and services through differentiating internal processes, including R&D, production, marketing, HR, and finance. The business is not componentized but semiintegrated through cross-functional processes, matrix structures, and management budgeting and control systems.

A value web includes multiple companies. For example, Li & Fung's suppliers play a dynamic partnership role in their relationship with Li & Fung; they choose to operate in its value web because they see it as a win-win situation. Small companies gain benefits that they could not obtain on their own; in return, they offer flexibility that Li & Fung could not build in a one-company value chain. The web works in parallel, not sequential, mode; it is integrated and agile, responding quickly to customer choices, partner priorities, and value web coordination. Effective value webs *start* with the customer, pulling together the right components to meet the market demand. The capabilities are componentized and integrated by the business platforms of the participants. None of the suppliers need to know anything about the others; the platform itself coordinates their individual components.

Within a value web, your business capabilities are limited only by your firm's platform and the platforms of your customers and partners. Those are very broad constraints, particularly in comparison with a value chain. There are multiple ways to grow by leveraging your platform, because you can build your own value webs and become a valued participant in other webs simultaneously. Options are unlimited, and business becomes unbounded. Costco and Amazon may or may not win as they expand into financial services, gourmet foods, jewelry, or appliances, but these spaces are open to them. For most companies, their spaces are both closed and their dimensions constrained by customers, commoditization, and the economy. Value web–based companies grow regardless of the economy.

A company whose value chain is under threat tends to close up and improve its productivity by cutting costs and, in the world of commoditization, its prices. Many factory-sector executives say that their best hope is to "hunt for nickel-and-dime savings." Where would

Cemex be if this were its leadership perspective? Part of an industry with less than 1 percent annual productivity growth. What happens when phone companies cut prices from 20 cents a minute to 10, then to 5, then to 2, then give away free minutes? What happens when any company cuts its own costs by 20 percent and moves along the same path of responding to competitive price reductions? After it reduces costs to zero, an impossible goal, its only option is to go out of business.

By contrast, what are the growth limits for Wal-Mart? A few years ago, its challenge was to reach $100 billion in sales. It is now at the $250 billion level and growing. Obviously, the Wal-Mart universe will not expand forever, but none of us know its growth limits, because it still has many value webs to weave, and its platforms remain as powerful as ever.

Integrate Your Components End-to-End to Deliver Platform Capabilities

The first management principle, described in Chapter 3, "It's All About Components," begins the platform-building sequence: Componentize your business. Componentization creates the building blocks. Our second management principle guides the development of the business platform that fits the building blocks together: *Integrate your components end-to-end to deliver platform capabilities.*

Each term here is chosen carefully.

- **Integrate to develop value web.** In a traditional value chain, companies seek to streamline their processes to make them more efficient. Streamlining is linear in its focus, however, and very much the target of value *chain* improvements through total quality management, business process reengineering, and business process management tools. Value webs make these useful but tactical operational developments on demand. An integrated web works in parallel and dynamically, via modular linkages. As eBay CEO Meg Whitman has stated more than once, eBay's success is based on its being a large, dynamically self-regulating economy.

- **End-to-end** refers to one of the most distinctive and far-reaching consequences of a platform-centered view: ending the dichotomy among the supply, demand, and administrative functions within a business. Supply chain "management" should be the coordination, on demand integration, of the capabilities that ensure the best customer service. Customer "service" should also be the on demand coordination of all upstream activities, including logistics and downstream selling and support operations. As we discussed in Chapter 4, "Creating Business Components," the customer service failures of eToys and Toys "R" Us were caused largely by supply chain problems and the disconnect between customer demand and supply capability response.

- **Capabilities** are the result of componentization and platform building. You can outsource the call center and reduce cost, or you can integrate someone else's call center components to improve time and quality while cutting costs, thus increasing your own capabilities. You can use UPS's shipping components as your own shipping department, as eToys did, or you can leverage them to deliver additional customer value, as Amazon does, and make shipping a value-added service. The choice is yours. The platform simply creates these opportunities.

A simple example of turning components into capabilities is the FedEx web site. Any customer can initiate a transaction and track a package end-to-end. This is a componentization of FedEx's internal tracking process, but by decomposing it—making it componentized, reusable, and transferable—FedEx has lowered its own costs and created a valuable customer service. It did not advertise online package tracking, yet within days, secretaries, small businesses, and office managers were tracking millions of packages. FedEx decomposed its value chain to turn processes into components and then delivered new capabilities via its existing platform. The customer becomes a collaborator. Without the platform that coordinates the movement of all the packages, however, this capability would not be possible.

Not stated, but absolutely necessary, is the concept of win-win-win. Participation in a value web is voluntary. With components and platforms, customers and suppliers have new options. Componentization allows them to exercise these options very quickly, and they will do so unless there is some extra value in not switching. Value webs demand relationships whereby every party gains something: the customer, the company, and its value web partners. Two out of three is not enough. Componentization of information and transaction processing via the Internet in airlines led to big wins for customers and such companies as Expedia and Travelocity, but the airlines were largely losers, as the other parties used their information to locate the best deals. Supply chain management is a zero-sum game whereby leading retailers played their suppliers off against one another, and even the B2B marketplaces that have transformed logistics still rely on mutuality of benefit.

This isn't to say that the gains are shared equally in value webs coordinated by such companies as Dell or Wal-Mart, however. Both companies make tough demands on their suppliers—that is the edge that a value web coordinator has over other members. But value webs are invitational—their scale, growth, and success rest on communication, coordination, collaboration, and that most elusive of values: trust. If they are not based on win-win-win principles, value webs are unstable, and companies begin to defect. Consider Covisint, a B2B marketplace proposed by large carmakers at the peak of the dot-com surge. The largest and most tightly linked suppliers recognized the benefits of scale and coordination, but the tier 2 suppliers—the ones that are less favored and more transaction focused—saw Covisint as a squeeze play and said "No thanks," dooming the venture.[9]

> *The choice of where to concentrate resources can be a bet-your-company decision.*

If your firm componentizes its value chain only in areas where it has tight control, you'll gain productivity benefits but run the risk of constraining your growth to what can be generated internally. If you aim to build growth primarily through participation in value webs woven and coordinated by others, you must stay in the mainstream of standardization; otherwise, you cannot move in harmony with your partners. At the same time, weaving your own web is easier said than done.

The dot-com failures and successes illustrate the risks inherent in building a branded portal. For every Amazon, Yahoo!, Schwab, or Dell, there are dozens of bold efforts that failed.

Participation in value webs and coordination of a firm's own webs are not either/or choices, but it takes organizational strength and resources to do both. Companies as diverse as IBM, GE, and Amazon have done so by componentizing the value chains that drive their core operations and then transforming the chains into value webs whereby they own the brand. At the same time, they look for opportunities to participate in other value webs. In every single instance, they create their capabilities via their platforms: systematic, coordinated, and integrated springboards for efficient operations, phased expansion, and focused innovation. The discipline required to do so is substantial, but the chaos of ad hoc, fragmented, case-by-case, function-by-function, and process-by-process development is far more costly in the long run.

Circuit City labored for years to release a home-grown point-of-sale system. When its new CIO realized that the system had only 30 percent of the required functionality and was deployed in only 16 percent of stores nationwide *five years* after beginning the project, the company canceled the project and switched to a standardized, component point-of-sale solution.[10]

UPS: Creating New Capabilities
That Others Value

UPS componentized its business and built a platform so that it could participate in a variety of value webs that others wove. This platform is an integral part of many firms, whether in the consumer or business-to-business marketplace. In fact, more than 60 percent of all items sold via the Internet are shipped through UPS.[11] UPS goes well beyond handling only pickup and delivery; it has evolved to being a third-party logistics leader. The very term *third party* highlights its role in value webs. Whereas Li & Fung is at the center of a value web, controlling the coordination rules and relationships, UPS is open to business, anyone's business. How tightly customers choose to link to UPS is the difference between using its services on a transaction basis and building a value web that incorporates UPS components and turns them into new capabilities.

UPS has added to its platform many components that permit new forms of operational integration. Here are just a few examples.

- UPS took over the management of replacement-parts inventory for IBM, Compaq, and Dell by managing their stock in a nationwide complex of warehousing and end-to-end logistics coordination that ensure that technicians can get a part within four hours.

- 1 Basketball, a manufacturer of basketball clothes and sneakers, relies on UPS's Supply Chain Solutions unit (SCS) for its entire back-office operations. "We feed our orders to them electronically and they fill them."[12] That covers shipping product directly to SCS's facility in Kentucky, warehousing it, and delivering it to such retailers as Foot Locker.

- SCS also handles reverse logistics for its clients. When a digital projector made by InFocus Corporation in Oregon breaks down, the customer sends it back to SCS in Kentucky, where UPS employees repair and return it.

- Minnesota-based Fender manufactures high-end guitars, and it cut delivery time by a week and reduced its distribution costs by almost 10 percent by cosourcing its entire logistics-management processes with UPS: order fulfillment, warehousing, investment management, delivery, and set-up service. All Fender's goods are delivered from a UPS warehouse in Maastricht, the Dutch transportation hub that has made this small country a center of international trade. Prior to Fender's relationship with UPS, one of the main sources of cost and delays was the requirement that a professional musician tune each guitar. That is now handled by a team of musicians who work in UPS's Maastricht warehouse, instead of customers contacting Fender to schedule a local musician.[13]

This is much more than simply outsourcing your shipping; it is adding important new capabilities through the value web firms' collaboration, processes, computer and telecommunications systems, and creative thinking. It adds significant value to customer relationships and enables the firms to improve their customer service while *removing* facilities and processes. It is win-win-win—a win relationship for the client, its customers, and the business partner provider.

Value Webs Provide Options

The reason so many value web players are fairly new and heavily dependent on online services is that they have a modern technology base that allows them to maximize their capabilities. It is no coincidence that the explosion in global sourcing came when—for the very first time—the Web provided firms with a set of standardized communications protocols, interfaces, and web pages. These opened up immediate opportunities for firms to interface services and operations. The continuous flow of new Web Services standards and tools will liberate enterprise technology from in-house systems and dependence on specific vendors and software. The new era is here.

Of course, that doesn't mean that economic cycles are going away. There are also industry aberrations that go far beyond normal economic cycles. Savvy executives recognize when they are in those aberrations and know that they don't last. The stock market bubble of the late 1990s was one of those aberrations. More recently, the mortgage business has seen another. With unusually low interest rates, banks raised their holdings of residential mortgages by some $125 billion, and home-equity loans soared by 36 percent. To handle these loan volumes, lenders have built up huge infrastructures and hired 120,000 additional people since 2001.[14] As interest rates rise, lenders will have to reduce those infrastructures and release many of the people.

But what if these companies had sourcing options?

Industry Decomposition—Not "If" but "Who Wins?"

There is a natural evolution from an individual company looking to improve its internal operations to the transformation of an entire industry. Initially, the smart firm decomposes its value chain into components and seeks to cut its fixed costs and reduce management distraction. This is what we call the get-ready-to-outsource phase. The proactive firm then focuses on building a platform that integrates its many elements, mindful that the main difference between components and platform is *coordination*.

The need for coordination increases rapidly as business logic pushes the firm toward a demand focus, gaining the adaptability and flexibility to sense and respond to changes in the ecosystem. As more and more companies make this move, the nature of competition and industry economics shifts toward variable-cost sourcing and scaling instead of fixed-cost in-house operations. This creates the commoditization cycle described in Chapter 2, "Commodity Markets Defined," whereby margins drop as price pressures and overcapacity fuel commoditization, which stimulates more decomposition of the value chain as companies look to outsource noncore functions.

In the *control phase* of the move toward componentization, firms do not invent new coordination mechanisms; they rationalize and streamline their existing operations. That is why the most immediate moves are to outsource functions that are already fairly independent of internal operations and can therefore be cut off from the organization without impacting strategic processes. Obvious examples are call centers, many manufacturing activities, travel services, shipping, and routine information technology functions. The easier it is to connect to providers, the faster the shift. The convenience of shipping via UPS and FedEx is also an example, with the caveat that including it in the integration of end-to-end capabilities is a very different discipline that rests on coordination and collaboration. Stated more bluntly, eToys is gone because it treated shipping as a separate and disconnected activity, and Amazon is very much in business.[15] Unlike eToys, Amazon understood that its business depended on being able to coordinate the fulfillment process end-to-end such that promises were not made that could not be met. Amazon assumed responsibility for the entire supply chain, including shipping functions that others performed.

The Automobile Industry: Decomposition and Value Web Formation

The auto industry also exemplifies the link between platform and collaboration. BMW's arrangement with Magna Steyr to handle every element of the manufacturing of its X3 SUV illustrates the shift from internal componentization to value web development based on relationship skills. Magna's team of engineers spent four weeks training at BMW's plants, "immersing themselves in BMW's products and culture, right down to how a Bimmer drives,"[16] and then pioneered a new four-wheel drive system for the X3 and adapted its data networks to interface with BMW's supply chain systems and to handle custom orders.

Contract manufacturing has been commonplace for years, especially in consumer electronics and appliances. The challenge that BMW faced was to reduce capital expenditures while simultaneously extending its styles and products. The company is now adding a new model every three *months*; five years ago, BMW saw product gaps of three years between models. The relationship with Magna reflects one of the most typical, perhaps even prototypical, payoffs from the component-platform strategy as a strategic focus: BMW's engineers are now free to add new models and help the company grow.

Magna provides component-based services for many other car manufacturers. Saab has contracted with it to engineer and produce a new convertible. Magna had earlier taken over engineering of the Audi TT and produced cars for Volkswagen and Mercedes. In 1998, Mercedes asked Magna how quickly it could set up a new production line to meet surging demand for its M-class SUV, and "Magna put it together in eight months—breakneck speed for the industry."[17]

Win-win-win relationships, speed, on demand scaling, simplification, focus, cost variability, quality—and growth. Again and again, these same value web factors are the drivers of decomposition. It may take years to fully evolve, but once it reaches critical mass, the industry is changed forever. This is most apparent in consumer electronics and personal computers, but there are obvious hints of the same inevitability in the BMW example. In the car industry, Magna Steyr dominates where it provides services in emerging value webs that are growing in scale and scope, even while other players are entering the field, often in specialized roles, such as design engineering. If BMW, the very acme of industry performance and consumer reputation, moves toward collaborative sourcing—cosourcing rather than outsourcing—and if Mercedes, Porsche, Volkswagen, and other top brands are also doing so, surely the rest of the industry will have to follow. Contract manufacturers, parts providers, design engineering firms, and other parts of the business ecosystem must adapt to standardization and relationship changes if they are to be part of the resulting value web.

Recomposition and Value Webs

Recomposition begins when an industry becomes largely standardized and differentiation becomes more and more the key to avoiding commoditization. Differentiators fit all the pieces together in new ways, with value webs as the main driver. In retailing, supply chain capabilities are the foundation of operations. In financial services, relationship excellence makes a Charles Schwab stand out in an industry in which many companies offer the same products and services. Consumer financial services products are almost all just a commodity component in its transaction features: credit cards, mortgages, consumer services, insurance, stocks, and even mutual funds. The industry is fueled by standardization, componentization, and industry decomposition.

> *Innovation in design, service, and relationships becomes the new differentiator.*

A lesson from the BMW/Magna relationship is that *making* cars will soon vanish as a differentiator.

In all industries, the effective individual company response to recomposition is to move toward end-to-end integration. Wal-Mart has powerful integrated information technology platforms that interface parties along the entire demand cycle, from customer to company to supplier base to partnerships. They share many of the very same business components as their competitors.

Wal-Mart relies on interfacing in all its activities. Its contracts with suppliers are relationship—not transaction—centered and are geared to end-to-end integration. Examples of its leadership include point-of-sale data sharing, whereby key suppliers have real-time information on product sales by item, size, and store, and vendor-managed inventory, whereby they stock the shelves themselves. Collaborative forecasting based on information sharing along the manufacturing, supply, and distribution chain enables each player to reduce inventories by up to 25 percent.[18] Wal-Mart will further shorten reporting lag by deploying RFID (radio frequency identification) tags that update the POS data resource as the goods are delivered to the store and as they pass the cash register scanner when bought.

eBay: The Platform as the Business

One company that took brilliant advantage of the new component technology is eBay. Perhaps no firm more clearly and convincingly indicates the value of platform-based business as the basis of value web innovation. CEO Meg Whitman describes her firm's strategy as "a marketplace that connects buyers and sellers. Fundamentally, eBay provides a global online trading platform where anyone can trade anything." Whitman really emphasizes the extent to which eBay is a network, a trading "community." It has continuously extended its value web, creating immense new opportunities for small businesses. "Spread across the globe—from The Peoples' Republic of China, Germany, and Argentina to the United States—they have almost 200,000 full-time eBay sellers." As Whitman says: "Before eBay and before the Net, small businesses in particular were constrained by geography. If you owned a small shop in San Francisco, your trading area was largely people who lived in that general area. That's not true today."[19]

Meg Whitman describes eBay as *fundamentally* built to operate on demand. Her firm has close to a hundred million customers "who expect us to be up 24 by 7, and their needs are constantly changing. Our industry is incredibly dynamic, and we have to be the fastest moving, most flexible, most single focused, and very simple company, actually. Yes, we provide the trading platform, but it is actually our community of users who every day list 22 million items for sale. They do their own customer support, they do their own pick, pack, and ship."[20]

The platform is the strategy, and it has become a growth machine. "The other thing that we've increasingly seen over the last couple of years is how the platform is able to enable economic opportunity around the world. For sellers, it broadens their market opportunity." In the last quarter of 2003, 12 percent of all transactions on eBay were between a buyer and a seller in different countries.

Whitman acknowledges the advantage gained from starting out in the new-technology environment of the Internet, which eBay used as the foundation of a synchronized and standardized platform. She also views strategic organizational priorities very much in the same way that Jeff Immelt does: "The good news is we don't have a lot of legacy systems. We got to build [the platform] from the ground up. But we did it every day with an eye toward driving simplicity and efficiency into this system, how we maximize the people that are helping our community build the business and minimize overhead."

"It takes an attitude and it takes a discipline and it takes an underlying technology that allows your product development staff to do the 'and' of product velocity *and* product quality. And the single most important decision we made was for one global trading platform, one internationalized code base. You cannot possibly do 27 countries where every country has different features, different functionalities, different user interfaces. But then you sit with the country manager in China who says it has to be different for me. And what we have tried to do is standardization. Yes, the local HTML, the local categories are obviously driven by the country management. But the code base is universal. And fortunately we made that decision because we would be in a bad situation at the moment if we had 27 different sites around the world."[21]

Now, eBay is the largest online trading platform in the world. Initially, it was put together on a fairly ad hoc basis, not through focused platform design. In mid-1999, this led to a loss of service that put the company at substantial risk; its share price dropped 50 percent in less than a week. The system, as it existed, did not scale to meet its demand. Management discipline plus new componentized technology have now given eBay an edge. Its users list 22 million items each day and make 7.5 million bids. The company sends 17 million outbound e-mails a day. The volume of data transmitted grows almost exponentially. Here is Meg Whitman's explanation of why this is no longer a problem: "It's a distributed, modularized, componentized database." Business components and technology components go together.

Because of the online nature of its business and lack of a legacy organization, eBay gains all the advantages of componentization. It has no inventory or warehouses and no sales forces or commissions. It also has "extraordinarily low capital requirements." Ninety-eight percent of eBay's capital expenditure is for technology. Because it is such a low-capital-intensity business, it generates a lot of cash, even though "we don't need cash to grow." That last comment captures what may well prove to be a mantra for building successful businesses in this on demand world.

What stands out among these business leaders is not that they have any specific strategic insight, proprietary advantage over their competitors, or share some common business model but rather that they *configure* their businesses with components and platforms and create new and enhanced capabilities through their value webs. Companies whose leaders provide governance directives, policies, and a process and technology base that's built on standardized interfaces have options. The players that are not built upon componentized platforms do not. In industry after industry, it is as basic as that.

GE, eBay, Amazon, UPS, FedEx, Wal-Mart, Swiss Re, and the other examples we've discussed are very different in their industries, strategies, markets, and customer base. But they are all leaders because for all of them, the platform is the strategy and components are its capability base.

We have focused on the move from decomposition to platform and from value chain to value webs. One of the most effective extensions of value generation is the topic of our next chapter: expanding your growth space by linking your business platform to partners, creating new value webs. Components and platforms enable innovation, *componentized value chains* facilitate internal innovation, and value webs facilitate *shared* innovation.

Summary

Creating a componentized business accomplishes little unless you ensure that your firm integrates these components across its value web via a business platform. This is done through standard interfaces, governance, policies, rules, and funding. Much is drawn form the analysis of industry leaders Cemex, Toyota, and eBay, firms that are at the leading edge of platform integration with their global infrastructures.

6

EXPAND YOUR
GROWTH SPACE

Li & Fung built a value web with thousands of suppliers, each providing a specific component, such as fabric manufacturing, dyeing, sewing, buttons, yarn making, packing, and shipping. It is able to charge handsomely for its services and has taken over more and more planning and logistics for such clients as the Gap, Calvin Klein, and The Limited. Hong Kong–based TAL Apparel has built an equally effective value web, one that makes 12.5 percent of all dress shirts sold in the United States.[1] It, too, is very profitable and has a strong reputation for entrepreneurship. Both companies are expanding across their entire business ecosystem of geography, services, and partners. Neither of them brands the end product but instead strengthens client brands and customer service. And they grow and grow.

Apparel is a horrendously tough business for both manufacturers and retailers. Retail prices affect what manufacturers can charge, and for basic apparel goods, prices have been flat or declining for more than a decade. TAL has seen its own prices fall by 20 percent in five years. Levi Strauss, once the producer of premium-price jeans, no longer manufactures in the United States and now must survive in a competitive environment in which the average price of jeans dropped from $40 in 1998 to $34 in 2003, with large retail chains selling them at $24. In late 2002, the last major U.S. shirt-making facility closed down. Competitive intensity is ever-increasing, owing to three interacting forces: globalization, deregulation, and technology.

Technology enables scattered operations to be globally coordinated; both TAL and Li & Fung invest heavily in their technology platforms, which fuel their globalization as country after country moves to expand its activities. In fact, whereas East Asian growth in apparel making has been fairly flat in recent years, the Caribbean has been increasing capacity at 30 percent per annum.

> ## *Deregulation drives increased globalization.*

The World Trade Organization mandated an end to textile quotas, which has led to aggressive expansion in such countries as India and Indonesia.

The Internet has also become a contributor to competitive intensity, with Amazon as one of its leaders: In late 2002, Amazon announced that it was teaming up with the Gap, Lands' End, Nordstrom, and Target to offer more than 400 popular brands in its Apparel and Accessories Store. This store includes all the features of Amazon's platform, including buyer reviews, catalogs, search, and price-comparison services.

The impact of this competitive intensity on the ecosystem is overcapacity everywhere, particularly because, in the apparel industry, componentization is a natural by-product of technology. Instead of manufacturing a shirt, as was the case in the heyday of the textile industry, companies like Li & Fung assemble it, often by coordinating dozens of factories scattered across the globe. TAL goes one step beyond in its relationship with JC Penney because TAL decides what to make and then tells JC Penney what the retailer has bought.

These two Hong Kong–based companies—TAL and Li & Fung—built growth engines in an industry that is truly commodity hell. TAL CEO Dr. Harry Lee transformed the business from a Take Control to a Let Go strategy, a more nimble and successful response to commoditization for both TAL and its customers. This process was not easy or quick to accomplish. TAL's Take Control strategy had failed; it had relied on a U.S. wholesaler that handled its shirts, so when that company went bankrupt, TAL bought it, but TAL's managers did not understand the wholesaling business—within three years, TAL had lost $50 million on the acquisition and shut the company down. Dr. Harry Lee said that the firm lost its "pants and underwear" trying to brand TAL goods in the marketplace.[2] TAL's effort to sell branded items in the United States through acquiring a Mexican factory met the same fate.

In the 1980s, TAL shifted its business strategy to help other companies work more effectively rather than remain trapped as a low-cost supplier. It built the foundation of its value web through investments in supply chain management and logistics services, enabled by information technology. This made TAL a strong supplier: Clients placed orders and TAL fulfilled them. The company built a strong relationship with retailer JC Penney and, in mid-1995, established a new service whereby it could replenish Penney's stock in one week, a dramatic improvement over the industry standard of six months. This was a remarkable accomplishment, but other firms were catching up on basic supply chain management.

Spanish clothier Zara had also shortened store replenishment to days and introduced 12,000 different designs a year. The Swedish company Hennes & Mauritz learned to treat fashion goods as if they were "perishable produce: keep it fresh and keep it moving."[3] H&M outsourced production to a huge network of 900 factories in 21 countries and focused on speeding up design; it can now move a garment from concept to store floor in as little as three weeks.

Both Zara and H&M have built a successful growth platform to meet their own needs. Zara has close to 1,000 stores and makes most of its products in Spain. H&M has grown its number of stores by 75 percent in six years and commands gross margins of more than 50 percent; same store sales are increasing by 4 percent to 5 percent a year. Whether the two companies can sustain growth is uncertain in the volatile fashion industry. The Gap, once the hottest chain in the United States, struggled abroad; the Body Shop slipped into a struggle-and-reconstruct situation after years of tremendous growth. Both built strong value chains and must continue to keep control of them to maintain their edge. As many have found, they can rapidly expand at first, through opportunistic site location and franchising, but then run out of expansion space, sometimes literally so, when franchisees find that the franchise has opened another store in their region. The value chain has a relatively fixed length.

TAL uses a different business model: a value web rather than a value chain. TAL CEO Dr. Lee explains that he learned from the firm's failed acquisition of its U.S. wholesaler that inventory management and matching supply to demand were the critical competitive needs, not just product. He saw that JC Penney was warehousing up to nine months of shirt inventory, shirts that were going out of style as they sat. This stock level was twice that of Penney's main competitors. To solve this supply chain failure, he proposed on a visit to Penney's headquarters that TAL supply shirts directly to stores instead of sending bulk orders to JC Penney warehouses.

The idea was quickly rejected, and each division of JC Penney had its own objections. Primarily, warehousing said it would be a disaster if TAL did not deliver the right goods to the right store on schedule, whereas IT worried about incompatibilities between the two computer systems. Years later, a new commitment to reducing inventories across JC Penney led to the plan's being revived and successfully piloted. A few months later, TAL was delivering shirts directly to all of Penney's North American stores, and inventories dropped immediately.

The next idea that Lee proposed was the value web leap. Why not have the TAL staff in Hong Kong forecast how many shirts each store would need each week? Penney's existing sales forecasts were often missed, sometimes dramatically overestimating demand and other times resulting in stockouts of fast-moving items. TAL reasoned that if it could get sales data straight from the stores, it could monitor the customer's pulse and respond instantly to any changes, ordering more fabric and increasing production where needed.

The results have been dramatic: zero inventory for Penney's in-house shirt brands.[4] TAL will make and send even one custom-made shirt to a store. JC Penney also let go of design and handed it over to TAL. TAL's New York and Dallas teams now come up with a proposed design and within a few months produce and test market 100,000 new shirts. Not all will sell, but the system lets customers, not marketing managers, choose what to buy. A JC Penney executive comments, "When we can put something on the floor that the customer has already voted on, that's where we make a lot of money."[5]

TAL is now the world's largest shirt maker. It has extended its value web to add services in the nonphysical areas of logistics. Because its technology platform is highly componentized and built on industry interface standards, it has also been able to quickly incorporate new software that enables electronic transactions, replacing the costly trade financing processes that added almost $250 to the cost of each order.

TAL invests in R&D that has led to several industry-leading innovations that it now licenses; a widely praised example is its Pucker-Free seam technology, which greatly improves wrinkle-resistant, noniron shirts. Brooks Brothers was an early adopter of this technology.

> *Platform companies focus their R&D and process innovations to benefit both themselves and their value web partners.*

TAL is successful because JC Penney let go. The degree of power that JC Penney turned over to TAL is radical. "You are giving away a pretty important function when you outsource your inventory management. That's not something a lot of retailers want to part with."[6] In return, TAL also lets go of many common suppliers' rules. For example, TAL will occasionally misestimate a store's requirements. When that happens, TAL picks up the extra cost for shipping by air instead of sea. It synchronizes its main factories in Asia, together with a garment factory in Mexico and a weaving and spinning mill in North Carolina, along with its many suppliers of buttons, zips, thread, fabric, and so on. These components are assembled to provide a commodity good, and the result is that JC Penney pays no price premium for its house brands.

Were the shirt-retailing business not so continually pressured by commoditization, there would be little incentive for JC Penney to let go. Were the industry not so componentized, TAL's strategy of fitting the component pieces together would not be practical. Without its growth platform, TAL would have to compete on a control-based strategy in an increasingly difficult business market, but instead, it has growth options everywhere. Ashworth, the leader in "golf-inspired" sportswear, views TAL as key to its being able to keep ahead of commodity competitors. TAL remains a success owing to its new capabilities in such areas as trade financing, opportunities to extend its platform into the Asian consumer market and to European customers, and through its distinctive role in helping clients do their own businesses better.

TAL's value web is a success and a growth engine *because* of commoditization, not in spite of it.

Where Is Your Firm's Growth Engine?

TAL and JC Penney are both letting go, yet they have different growth platforms. How, then, does a company identify its own platform? By answering one question: Where will our growth come from? We suggest that there are five pivotal choices. We use "pivotal" because they are the focus—the pivot point—for defining strategic intent and hence the governance, interface standards, and synchronicity of the platform. They are pivotal also in that the choice is crucial and consequential.

Each of the five types of growth platforms can be described by an action: control, coordinate, service, collaborate, and enable. Table 6.1 defines these pivot points and the growth associated with each.

Table 6.1   Pivot Points

Growth Platforms	
Pivot Points	Where the Growth Comes From
Control	Your traditional value chain (in-house capabilities plus M&As)
Coordinate	Your value web (coordination of capabilities—yours and your partners')
Service	Your partners' value webs (your innovation and coordination of your capabilities on behalf of your selective partners)
Collaborate	A wide range of value webs (services offerings that others find irresistible to add to their value webs)
Enable	New or expanding value webs (opening your platform, inviting others to innovate on their own behalf)

Let's explore each in more detail.

- **Control**—In the power-player model, growth comes from per-
fecting the traditional value chain, growing and managing in-
house capabilities, along with mergers and acquisitions. Just
about everything is proprietary. There is very little letting go
and little growth; the control model has a pretty dismal growth
record in that regard. A few companies are still able to make it
work, though (Southwest Airlines being an excellent example).

- **Coordinate**—Growth comes from the ability to build a value
web and coordinate a wide range of component capabilities,
both the firm's own and those provided by expanding its access
to outside relationships. The imperative is to build your own
value web, making effective use of partners and of creative,
rather than reactionary, sourcing models. This is the blueprint
for most large companies. P&G is an example of a formerly
control-focused company that has made the shift to coordination. Coordinating companies rely on synchronization of relationships but on their own terms. They let go through their
strong focus on coordinating value web relationships, especially
in supply chain management. This is clearly where JC Penney is
heading. The major challenge in making the shift from control
to coordination is getting the culture to let go and become truly
collaborative. (We explore this key aspect of organizational
mobilization in Chapter 8, "From Vision to Results: The
Leadership Agenda.")

- **Service**—Firms grow by innovating and coordinating their
own capabilities on behalf of partners. Firms build tight relationships with selected clients and grow as their partners move
from control to coordination and thus expand their value
space. Examples are Magna and Timken in manufacturing,
Flextronics and Solectron in electronics, TAL and Li & Fung in
retailing, and IBM and Accenture in IT and business processes.
Service-platform companies grow through their contributions
to a componentized ecosystem. It is not coincidental that
service-platform firms are proliferating in highly commoditized

ecosystems, such as car manufacturing and consumer electronics, or that few are household names. These component "suppliers" offer more than simply supplying things. They even give up their own brands because they are part of a coordinated value web owned by the client. The combination of coordination brand players and service-component platform specialists is exemplified in the relationships between JC Penney and TAL, BMW and Magna, and even the HR services that IBM manages for P&G; they generate innovation through components, allowing brand players to get out of the commoditization bind. Their skill is in relationship management, increasingly the differentiator in any commodity business.

- **Collaborate**—A firm grows through dynamic value web participation by offering a range of services to any client/cosourcer/partner. FedEx, IBM, and UPS are exemplars in this regard. Collaborative firms offer such services as shipping, payroll processing, call center expertise, and IT operations, providing generic components rather than the industry-specific offerings of service-platform companies. They profit and grow by offering the same service to a wide range of customers, their key organizational skill is sales, and their core platform priority is synchronization and reliability of service.

- **Enable**—A small number of very skilled value web players add to their growth and open their platform capabilities by inviting others to innovate on their behalf. Growth comes as these partners expand and reward the enabler, often in the form of commissions, referrals, and shared business. Amazon and eBay increasingly rely on new uses of their platforms that they do not initiate but enable. This is an extension of collaboration in that a firm with a distinctive set of platform capabilities offers some of its components to allow other firms to innovate. The enabler gains from fees, through partnerships, and in the creation of new value webs. IBM and P&G have turned their patent portfolios into very profitable licensed components available even to competitors.

These growth pivots are not mutually exclusive. The stronger the platform becomes, the more growth opportunities become available. Here we use *stronger* in terms of governance rules that expand collaborative roles, the range of standardized technology, process and service interfaces, and synchronicity, scale, reliability, and responsiveness. Remember that a growth platform can expand well beyond its own control spaces into new coordination spaces, service spaces, collaboration spaces, and innovation spaces. The driver of growth is *more* rather than *bigger*.

Letting Go: Moving from Control to Coordination

Coordination is the obvious pivot point and blueprint for most large companies. It is the natural evolution from the value chain to a value web because the company stays at the center of its own web. We've seen this move in several of our examples. A. G. Lafley is transforming P&G, based on the premise that it will "do what they are best at and nothing more."[7] P&G is outsourcing HR administration, IT operations, and the manufacturing of such products as Ivory soap. P&G is also strengthening its beauty products brands and expanding its value web to include healthcare products, such as the over-the-counter drug Prilosec.

Wal-Mart's move to coordination actually started with P&G. As Wal-Mart's founder, Sam Walton, described the story,[8] until the mid-1980s, Wal-Mart and P&G had a very adversarial relationship. P&G would dictate how much Wal-Mart would sell and at what price. Wal-Mart would, in turn, threaten to drop P&G products or give it bad shelf space. There was no sharing of data, joint planning, or systems coordination. A mutual friend arranged a canoe trip for Sam and Lou Pritchett, P&G's vice president of sales. On the trip, the two men decided to reexamine the adversarial relationship, starting with a top-executive joint-planning meeting. The result was a plan for Wal-Mart to share its point-of-sales data so that P&G could take responsibility for managing Wal-Mart's inventory. That plan not only changed the relationship between Wal-Mart and P&G but also reduced costs and improved operations for both companies. It also changed forever the way in which Wal-Mart runs its business. That was the starting point for Wal-Mart's componentization and coordination with a wide range of vendors. But first, both Wal-Mart and P&G had to relinquish control and build new coordination capabilities; 18 years later, Wal-Mart is still transforming.

In one of its most recent moves, Wal-Mart is requiring all vendors to put RFID tags on all pallets. At the same time, it is streamlining the distribution centers and working toward item-based RFID tags with shelf readers so that vendors don't simply manage inventory levels but can deliver directly to stores, refilling depleted shelves and bypassing the distribution centers completely. Wal-Mart should be able to double the volume of goods sold without building another distribution center, according to some industry analysts.

GE is focused on simplification, process entitlement, centralization, and outsourcing to free up resources for innovation. GE's role as a coordinator of its own value web is evident in GE Healthcare's centers of excellence. But GE is not merely a coordinator, remotely monitoring MR scanners in hospitals, turbines on ships, and railroad services that increase on-time operations. GE plays a service role in other companyies' value webs in addition to coordinating its own web. Like GE, IBM is known as a coordinator in the hardware and software business but increasingly plays the service role in other value webs for IT operations and HR administration.

Dell may be the best known of the value web coordinators, synchronizing a complex value web that includes many players. Yet Dell owns and operates very little of its "core" business and does almost no research. Like P&G and Wal-Mart, it has a much narrower focus than a traditional control player, but Dell also provides a glimpse of the future in which competitors start new businesses in ecosystems that have componentized or are in the process of componentizing. In an industry bifurcating between the high-value solutions providers and the lower-end component space, Dell has chosen to build its business upon industry-standard parts and components. Microsoft does the software R&D and recruits and coordinates thousands of application partners, Intel makes the microprocessors, and component manufacturers design and make printers, displays, memory chips, and motherboards. Dell couldn't afford to create every piece of the value chain, so Dell built a platform that synchronizes all activities, based on its direct-sell model.

The move to coordination is a natural one for control players, but it's not easy; it takes focus and discipline. As the world componentizes, more companies will enter an ecosystem that is already componentized and they won't go through the decomposition process.

More than Service with a Smile

Service-platform companies are built on commodity components that they augment in some way—generally through specialized, highly focused service and a commitment to quality. An exemplar in this regard is American Axle and Manufacturing. Its founder, Richard Dauch, played a major role as a top executive in Chrysler's rejuvenation in the 1980s. After he left Chrysler, Dauch scouted for new opportunities in manufacturing. One came from another of his previous employers, GM, which was busy restructuring and had put up for sale five old Detroit axle and drive-train plants. Some of the machinery was 40 years old, and the plants were in total disrepair.

And yet their components were critical for GM. Indeed, as part of the purchase agreement, GM agreed to keep buying most of the plants' output if quality was improved. In response, Dauch built a new service platform, with GM as its main client. Today, about 80 percent of AAM's total output is still purchased by GM, though AAM is rapidly adding new clients, including domestic and foreign truck makers. In addition to rebuilding and modernizing the plants, Dauch upgraded his employee base; a ninth-grade education had been the norm, and now the average employee has two years of college. The average age dropped from 50 to 39, and the workforce became more diversified, though still predominantly male. AAM has doubled productivity and has been profitable in every year of its decade-old existence, with sales of more than $4 billion. AT Kearney ranked it as the best financial performer among automotive parts tier I suppliers.

People are one key element of AAM's platform governance. Another is its Factory Information System, which monitors every aspect of operations.

Dauch is a stickler for measuring everything the company does, down to the micrometer scale for components, a level at which differences are invisible to the human eye. AAM grew largely with the surge in GM's light-truck business, an example of how clients' value web growth is the driver for service-platform growth. AAM has been able to bring jobs back from Mexico and win contracts for work previously done in China, both bucking the predominant trend in the automotive industry. Dauch says that he is building a low-cost country in Detroit.

Magna and Flextronics, described earlier, are paralleling AAM's path. They focus on services to a well-defined range of clients, compete on price—as they must in a commodity environment—but differentiate through added services. In AAM's case, the differentiator is quality management; for Magna, it is engineering and production expertise; and for Flextronics, scale, reliability, and low overhead. In each case, large manufacturers come to rely on them for commodity components that many other players can offer, but they add a platform capability that few can equal. They live with commoditization, focusing their innovation and capital investment on quality and process improvements.

By changing from suppliers to service linkers, Magna, Flextronics, TAL, Li & Fung, AAM, and IBM Global Services complement the moves of BMW, P&G, and JC Penney from *control* to *coordination*. Together, the companies create a symmetry of capabilities: GM gets quality at the best price, and AAM gets volume. JC Penney gets greatly improved inventory management and capital efficiency, and TAL gains growth. The result is the synchronization of a value web that in the old days could not exist. In the old days, don't forget, GM made almost all its own parts, JC Penney managed its own inventory, and BMW made its own cars. There is a growth engine that is allowing large companies to let go of their in-house operations model, as service-platform firms pick up more and more business on their behalf.

Most service firms also have to be coordinators of their own value web. They build and enhance components that differentiate them and let go of those that don't: If they retain ownership of components that don't differentiate them and are available on the open market, they waste capital and scarce management resources, reducing growth opportunities.

Creating Markets Through Collaboration

The notion of complementarity is extended from specialist component services to general-purpose ones that such companies as UPS, FedEx, First Data, and eBay have as their growth-platform strategy. These firms all fuel their growth through customer growth and play an active role in supporting that growth. If they were simply suppliers, they would grow or shrink with the overall economy, as most companies do. Instead, they exploit their platforms to offer partners and customers components that are flexible and enable innovation.

FedEx and UPS

Here are a few examples, many of which we discussed earlier, that have worked for FedEx and UPS.

- **Deploy components on demand, as needed**—Using FedEx or UPS requires no long-term planning or new facilities.

- **Contribute to coordination across the client value space**— Amazon is as much a shipping company as an order-fulfillment retailer, and its order-to-delivery processes are fully synchronized with FedEx and UPS.

- **Transform cost structures**—FedEx and UPS are variable costs to their customers.

- **Open up collaborative and service opportunities to create new capabilities**—Fender's new synchronization of its delivery and service for top-end guitars exemplifies this type of collaboration.

- **Add to customer flexibility and adaptiveness, creating specialized services for select customers**—HP offers printer repairs without ever being involved in the process. UPS does this by exploiting its core pick-up and delivery services, augmented by warehousing, parts inventory management, and repair technicians.

First Data

From the time that the first bank credit card was issued in 1951, Visa International, Inc., and MasterCard International, Inc., have dominated the credit card business. These two associations were formed by the member banks to provide card services, including brand marketing and back-office switching networks. They started out as a *service* for the banks, but in an effort to strengthen the brand, they exerted more control, limiting the cards that member banks could issue and mandating which cards retailers could handle. Times have changed, and with the bank consolidation of recent years, more than 50 percent of cards are issued by fewer than a dozen banks. The Internet has made it far simpler to build networks, and card-transaction volumes are also increasing rapidly with debit card transactions, the most rapidly growing segment of the market. Squeezed by lower profit margins and the transaction costs associated with paper-based debit card processing, retailers are actively looking for ways to reduce their transaction costs.

First Data offers these retailers a viable alternative. First Data was founded in 1992 when American Express decided to spin off its credit card processing operations as an independent company. Between 1992 and 2002, revenue increased by 500 percent and profits by 700 percent. Today, First Data provides card-processing services for more than 1,400 card issuers with 398 million accounts on file, processing 37 percent of all credit card transactions.[9] In early 2004, First Data completed the purchase of Concord EFS, giving First Data merchant services that enable millions of merchants worldwide to accept any type of electronic payment easily and securely. Today, First Data handles more than half of the PIN-debit transaction market through its Star network.

First Data offers banks card-processing services, and although it continues to expand those services, it also leverages its collaborative platform to offer banks additional services, such as cobranded cards, in competition with Visa and MasterCard. First Data can offer the banks a larger share of each transaction because of its efficient operations and expanding transaction volume. For the merchants, it offers a lower cost and more secure debit-card service. With the explosive growth in debit cards, First Data is leveraging that growth because of its platform and win-win-win approach to the game.

eBay

Illustrating the same principles of growth through collaboration, eBay provides a service that millions of customers use every day and leverages the *collaborative* pivot point to *enable* customer innovations through the use of its platform. For example, government agencies discovered that they could see as much as three times the price through eBay as they do with regular public auctions. Retailers use eBay to sell returned goods or to dispose of excess inventory. Many small businesses have transformed their own operations through access to the eBay technology and process platform (including payments, support, and training). The eBay chairman estimates that there are now well over 100,000 such small-scale entrepreneurs who use eBay as their business infrastructure. It is the infrastructure that differentiates eBay as collaborator and makes the firm much more than an auction transaction site.

BIG Ideas

Once large companies started to shift from control to coordination, many new value spaces opened up. Consider pharmaceutical research and development, whereby hospitals, companies, and individuals have become part of the value webs, and large firms cosource the innovation. Product development may not even be crucial to certain firms. Analysts Scott Anthony and Clayton Christensen[10] point to a small company, BIG (Big Idea Group), which acts as a link between "idea generators" and large companies looking for new-product opportunities in such industries as toy making, housewares, and do-it-yourself home improvements. BIG rents a conference room and invites in literally everyone interested in pitching their ideas to a panel of experts. It winnows the ideas and takes the best to potentially interested clients and then works with them to turn concept into product. BIG thus becomes a component in their larger enterprise capabilities and helps them think about innovation as a collaboration opportunity rather than as an in-house monopoly.

Enabling Customer and Partner Innovation

Through the use of its platform, eBay enables customer innovation. As its customers grow, eBay grows. The next extension of such collaboration is to explicitly make your own platform the enabler of customer innovation. Platforms have become an invitation to coordinate component capabilities, to offer services, to mutually benefit from collaborative linkages, and to invent.

The most intriguing innovator in this regard is Amazon. In a book that is focused on generating *profitable* growth, it may seem somewhat odd for us to pick Amazon as an exemplar. After all, it took a lot of investor capital to build the Amazon platform, and it took years for the company to be profitable. But Amazon is a platform company, and it has grown and grown. This is a $5 billion business built from scratch, in less than ten years. Had it been simply a dot-com and transaction machine, it probably would have failed. The company did make mistakes and has had to readjust its strategy more than once, but underlying Jeff Bezos's strategy has always been *platform*.

The core of the Amazon platform was its principle of becoming "the best place to find, discover, and buy any product or service available online."[11] This was the brand-building control stage of Amazon's business evolution. "We intend to leverage our Internet platform to expand the range of products and services offered to our customers"[12] became the story during the coordination stage. Our "third-party channel allows us to provide other companies with a set of e-commerce services and tools for the sale of their goods and services. We have third-party seller relationships with ToysRus.com, Inc.; Target Corporation; Circuit City Stores, Inc.; the Borders Group; Waterstones; Expedia, Inc...."[13]

Early in its development, Amazon tried to own relationships via equity positions in dot-coms, including drugstore.com, pets.com, and living.com. Most of those were unsuccessful but Amazon remains very much in business. Having evolved its strategy, it now offers a "home" to retailers, its thousands of associates, and technology innovators. Bezos never thought of Amazon as a bookseller or even a retailer but as an infrastructure. That infrastructure helped rescue Toys "R" Us and provided a viable way for Borders to "create" an Internet ordering channel without operating its own e-commerce site. Amazon now gets more than 20 percent of its unit sales, at a 15 percent commission, via other merchants. Amazon had already built the platform. These vendors help Amazon realize a bigger return.

Its most striking innovation was opening up its technology platform to outsiders. "Bit by bit, just like its Washington neighbor [Microsoft] did two decades ago, Amazon is building a platform: a stack of software on which thousands or millions of others can build businesses that in turn will bolster the platform in a self-reinforcing cycle."[14] Merchants are incorporating Amazon Web Services software into their own systems; more than 35,000 programmers have downloaded the free development kit. An example of business innovation via the Amazon platform is an individual who started selling books through Amazon in 2002. He then learned about an Amazon program that lets users scan a book's ISBN number and retrieve information on new and used sales. He can now instantly see the going price for any used book on Amazon and can use this information when he visits thrift stores or yard sales to pick out maximally profitable books. Using this information, he has more than doubled his revenues, from $100,000 to $250,000. That's what happens when you open your platform and invite your customers to innovate.

Amazon's growth comes from others' growth, as well as its own.

Where does your company's growth come from?

Growth Options and Opportunities

A business growth platform is an enabler, a springboard, a foundation, and a coordination mechanism. In and of itself, it does not generate growth, but it creates options that are not available to firms trapped in commodity hell. But you can't see these options until you truly let go to grow, because many are opportunistic and unpredictable, coming from shifts in the environment, new potential partnerships, and innovations in how business components are combined and deployed.

Here are just a few of the platform owner's growth advantages.

- Once a platform is in place, adding new capabilities is an incremental move instead of a strategic investment. That favorably transforms both risk and investment cost. It may take many years and hundreds of million of dollars to build a platform with the scale and capabilities of an Amazon, and it unquestionably demands sustained executive leadership to establish the governance rules and roles of a GE. Once in place and reliable, however, the platform will give you and your partners the flexibility needed to adjust to new demands in the ecosystem.

- Partnerships are then limited only by the standardized interfaces that the platform can support: technology interfaces, process interfaces, and customer interfaces.

- Growth is not limited to internal development. The most powerful way to create growth is through other companies' growth, via collaborations that provide mutual benefits. The platform also binds the partners so that there is less likelihood of a component-only player disrupting the relationship on the basis of price.

- The nature of innovation changes from something special and unique to a process of everyday opportunistic experimentation and advances along many process, service, relationship, and product fronts.

- Platform players have expanding and collaborative cosourcing options, to a degree that the term *outsourcing* becomes a misnomer. Cosourcing, the collaborative creation of value web-based process capabilities, whereby each player brings distinctive strengths, adds value; it doesn't reduce costs.

- New organizational structures and coordination processes can be quickly created to reflect the ever-evolving business ecosystem.

Lest we seem to be promising the moon, options are only options; they are not sure things. Our position is obviously one of advocacy, and we aim to convince you, our reader, that a platform-centered view of the growth opportunity is a necessity. There is danger, and at times we may underplay the complexities, uncertainties, and risks. Moreover, there are no guarantees in business, and although platform-based leaders have a decided edge in growth and innovation, other factors can erode or even cancel out that edge.

American Airlines dominated every area of innovation and performance in the 1970s through the early 1990s, with Southwest moving along a very different business-growth path. American's platform gave it an edge in launching the first frequent flyer program, and it was only American that for many years linked information across passenger, marketing, reservations, and planning. It was able to use this synchronized information as the base for its hubbing strategy. At the time, Chairman Robert Crandall stated that given the choice of selling off Sabre, its reservation system, or the airline, he would sell the airline.

Meanwhile, Southwest Airlines avoided hubbing in favor of point-to-point service along selected routes and standardized on a single plane, the Boeing 737, which reduced maintenance costs, simplified processes, and reduced inventory needs. It componentized its route structures, and its governance policies placed a huge emphasis on employee relationships because employees were the core of its platform. Southwest treated reservations as an operational commodity, whereas for American, it was a major element in its strategic innovation.[15]

In the early 1990s, American's operations platform was the base for its success, but in an era of change, flexibility is a key to success. In the airline business, change comes quickly, and successful platforms can be replaced by innovative new platforms overnight. Platforms wear out, and an operations platform does not generate growth, though it provides the functions and capabilities to move with growth. Operations platforms provide tremendous efficiencies and frequently grow over time. They often lack the flexibility required when major discontinuities occur, however.

Sabre Holdings Corp., spun off from American in 2000, has invested more than $100 million to transform its operational platform into a growth platform. It is creating a new way of doing business, a component-based platform that will enable Sabre to transition from a transaction service to a service value web, providing components that will enable travel agents to redesign their own businesses.

Southwest recognized early on the commoditized future and built a component platform that it leverages every day to grow.

Summary

Once you've created a flexible, integrated platform, profitable growth comes just as much from expanding into new market segments as being more efficient within your own segment. With the three interacting forces of deregulation, globalization, and technology comes greater competitive intensity too, so to be sustainable, growth must come from new market segments. The key question remains: Where is your firm's growth engine?

7

LIBERATE YOUR COST STRUCTURES

There are good revenues and bad ones. Good revenues build relationships, repeat business, and come with healthy gross margins, often owing to the firm's ability to differentiate products and services. This gives it both pricing power and the ability to continuously cut costs more quickly than its competition, without hurting relationships and repeat business. Bad revenues are simply commodity transactions that push the ecosystem toward even more price cutting as companies fight for market share. The sell-off of cars in the early 2000s at 0 percent financing arguably falls into the former category; telemarketing and mass mailings claiming "You have been preapproved for a new mortgage" clearly fall in the latter, bad-revenue category.

Whichever the case, growth should not come at the expense of profit. As well-known business strategist Peter Drucker puts it, profit is the cost of staying in business.[1] In a commoditized world with little pricing power, this means that cost rather than revenue is the real generator of profit. If you cut prices without cutting costs, profits are hurt. If your competitor cuts costs, along with prices, which of you will still be in business tomorrow?

If growth cannot come at the expense of profit, it also will not come from cutting costs. Cost cutting can increase short-term profitability, but it is basically a holding action until revenues can provide the leverage for profits. In the post-NASDAQ, post-9/11 era, with the rapid globalization of the early years of this new century, executives had no choice but to cut costs wherever they could. Cost cutting became the price of staying in business. But it is not a vehicle for growth. Cost cutting can stop the race for growth dead at the starting gate, when managers admit that they think a $10,000 idea could be worth a million in new business, but "budgets are frozen and any travel has to be preauthorized." The logic of business then shifts from "innovation at a sensible price" to "only costs count." It's the freeze of too much aversion to risk, and without risk, there is no growth.

In addition, whether made through mergers and acquisitions, reorganization, or competitive repositioning, aggressive-growth initiatives frequently generate massive restructuring costs—as much as 80 percent of profits for many Fortune 500 firms. Companies have to pay severance costs for laying off employees, employees who had been hired for the firm's future expansion. Facilities close, leases are canceled, and long-term assets are "withdrawn," which means that they are no longer assets but liabilities.

And yet, the most common executive response is to cut prices, hoping to maintain or increase revenues by taking market share. These dying firms hope that they can outlast their competitors, slash costs to increase profits, or buy revenue growth through acquisitions.

The Platform Solution: Changing Cost Structures

There is an alternative. Table 7.1 presents summary financial data from a Fortune 500 corporation. On the surface, there is reason for concern.

Table 7.1   Summary Financial Data

Company X Percentage Change 2000–2003	
	Percentage Change per Year
Overall revenue	+10
Revenue from acquisition	+4
Revenue from currency exchange rates	+7

(continues)

Table 7.1 *(continued)*

	Company X Percentage Change 2000–2003
	Percentage Change per Year
Revenue from organic growth	−1
Labor cost growth	+17
Price erosion	+12

Company X sees where high price erosion and high labor-cost growth, coupled with low overall growth, are leading and doesn't like it. That's why the firm is reinventing itself: Its new focus on collaborative relationships and selective outsourcing, cuts overhead costs by several billion dollars a year, and supply chain management initiatives reduce the incremental cost of supporting transaction volume growth by a few more billions. There is no way that this company's cost cutting will block the inevitable result of price erosion. This is not just cost cutting, however. The company is changing its cost *structures*. It is building a business platform that enables cost optionality, a balance between fixed and variable costs, coupled with choices about which processes to maintain in-house, which to outsource, and which to cosource.

The platform will likely be expensive to create, because there are many up-front costs that include process design and streamlining, facilitating cultural change, skill building, and information technology investments. Even with a platform, competitive intensity and the resulting ecosystem response produce continual price pressure. But the platform is enabling a long-term change in cost structures and revenue-growth opportunities. In this example, the company correctly recognizes that its productivity will not come from cost cutting but from a combination of cost optionality and new collaborations. Cost optionality helps it become more efficient through collaboration and more effective in its value web opportunities.

There are no two ways about it: Costs create or limit profits. Cost structures, by contrast, the balance between fixed- and variable-cost options, create or limit growth with profit. They can turn business expansion into immediate and sustainable profits. Platform companies are not locked into the cost profile of the traditional firm, and as component *users,* they can choose more and more variable-cost processes and services (as does P&G, for instance). As component *providers,* they can build fixed-cost platforms that exploit scale, specialized add-on skills, and low overhead to service multiple clients (Flextronics). In some instances, component providers can become trusted intermediaries coordinating entire component markets (Li & Fung).

This is the creative economy in action.

The BMW/Magna collaboration illustrates this duality, as do the JC Penney/TAL and P&G/IBM relationships. These transform the client's cost options for capital investment, scaling on demand (pay as you go for what you use, rather than pay up front), and component quality. It also creates an expansion space for the providers, though as they serve many clients, they must themselves take on many of the risks of their clients' now obsolete in-house value chain business model.

When business-growth opportunities become cost structure options too, this duality becomes extraordinarily powerful and has already led to a transformation of income statements and balance sheets of growth-platform leaders. Compared with their competitors, they use half the working capital per unit of sales, have half the GSA[2] overhead, and enjoy at least a similar edge in revenue per employee.

Growth-platform companies have four ways to leverage their cost/growth structures and avoid the trap of growth at the expense of cost efficiency, or cost cutting at the expense of growth.

1. Directly reduce costs through componentization.

2. Shift from fixed-cost operations to variable-cost components.

3. Leverage other firms' components.

4. Reduce restructuring costs.

Being able to combine *all* these cost structure options creates a significant competitive edge.

Directly Reduce Costs Through Componentization

Dell's 2003 revenues were a little more than half those of HP. The differences in financial metrics are presented in Table 7.2.[3]

Table 7.2   Dell versus HP Financials, Fiscal 2003

	Dell	HP	Dell/HP
Revenues	$35.4 billion	$73 billion	0.47
Operating profit	$2.84 billion	$2.89 billion	1.00
SG&A	$3.5 billion	$11 billion	0.32
Inventory	$0.3 billion	$6 billion	0.05
Plant and equipment	$0.9 billion	$6 billion	0.15

Every product that Dell sells is built on standard components, and it has never launched a creative innovation for the industry. Dell's net margin in its core personal computer business is just 3 percent, and its gross margins keep falling. Dell also remains a relatively small firm in its ecosystem, with 15 percent of the personal computer market and just a single-digit percentage of servers, storage, and peripherals. It spends just 1.5 percent of revenues on R&D, arguably a core investment for high-tech company innovation. Finally, Dell is also reducing prices by an average of 18 percent annually.

But the financials clearly show that Dell makes a lot of money, even as it drives ecosystem prices lower and lower. Whereas its gross margins drop and remain far below those of HP and other competitors, Dell's net margins maintain it as the industry leader in profitability.

Michael Dell has always stressed that his growth platform was based on componentization, reflecting his assumption of the inevitability of componentization in the high-tech business. Here are some of his most relevant observations, made back in 1998.[4]

Companies that were stars ten years ago, the Digital Equipments of this world, had to build massive infrastructures to produce everything a computer needed. They had no choice but to become expert in a wide array of components, many of which had nothing to do with creating value for the customer.

How can you grow so much faster without all those physical assets? There are fewer things to manage, fewer things to go wrong.

Outsourcing…is almost always getting rid of a problem a company hasn't been able to solve…. That is not what we are doing. We focus on how we can coordinate our activities to create the most value to our customers.

Dell could not have achieved this coordination without the rapidly emerging standardization of industry interfaces. Digital Equipment created the minicomputer and was a growth leader for several decades but it misread trends that Dell spotted and exploited. Digital bet its future on proprietary systems and products, the reverse of componentization, and fell from growth leader to takeover target as a result. By contrast, Dell let go, adopting Microsoft's operating system and the Intel microprocessor as its growth vehicle.

Had UNIX or Apple's Macintosh operating system become the standard or Motorola's CPU chips led the market, or had Dell tried to simultaneously support DOS, CPM, and UNIX, Dell's strategy would have failed, and Michael Dell's earlier statements would amount to an epitaph for a company that bet on the wrong platform.

The point we want to emphasize is the direct linkage between growth and cost structures. By cosourcing everything that it could, Dell minimized capital investment. There is an immediate saving here because inventory is not an asset but a drain on working capital. Facilities must be able to earn back their investment cost to justify their retention. A microprocessor chip fabrication plant, for example, may cost upward of a billion dollars to build and is costly to adapt to changing technologies. That's why Dell's philosophy is not to build but to use.

Dell's real growth began in 1996, when it began to use the Internet as a coordination platform for process components. Dell provided customized web sites for large customers that incorporated their business rules for procurement along with a wide range of self-management services, including product configuration, software downloading, and troubleshooting. Dell has more than 200 business-process patents—and no technology patents—and has so fine-tuned its supply chain that its inventory levels are the lowest in the industry, saving capital and enabling Dell to cycle new components into its products in less than two weeks.

By adding storage, servers, printers, and PDAs to its product line, Dell has deliberately targeted the commodity market and brought companies, such as EMC, and server, printer, and PDA makers onto its customer service and supply chain management platforms, effectively moving them into its commoditization machine. Dell did not have to acquire these companies. If their innovations create successful products, Dell also gains, yet it has very little risk if they fail, as they are only components.

Dell is best known for its inventory management. Inventory, of course, consists of goods that are bought before they are sold, which means that they have a carrying cost. This carrying cost is easily calculated as the weighted average cost of capital for the firm (the opportunity cost for tying up the funds) and the implicit "fee" that investors are charging the company. A firm that does not generate after-tax cash flows that exceed the cost of capital is draining shareholder value. Inventory does this; it is exactly like stashing a few thousand dollars in a mattress. It sits there and cannot be used profitably elsewhere.

The cost of capital for a well-run firm is in the range of 8 percent to 16 percent; so $1 million of inventory costs $30,000 for each quarter that it's held. In the meantime, the price the product commands may drop 2 percent—$20,000—or more. Lack of the process base to manage inventory thus provides what we refer to as a business-inefficiency penalty on the company of $50,000 per quarter. If the company's net margin is 5 percent, this means that the gross profit on the sale is wiped out by the inventory cost. That is not the way to grow. It was once but only as long as a company or industry could pass on its cost increases to customers.

Shifting Away from Fixed-Cost Operations

A business component—whether a process, a product, or a commercial service—is a variable-cost opportunity for a buyer and a revenue opportunity for a seller. That has truly profound consequences for business design and is the long-term force behind the growth in global sourcing. For the first time in business history, organizations can integrate components across geography, companies, and organizational functions *on any scale.*

An extreme example of a completely scale-free business is Yahoo!, which is a value web built on others' components: search engines, stores, financial services, news providers, business auctions, and hundreds of other services, more than would fit on a single page.

These informational components are all variable costs; Yahoo! owns none of them. Yahoo! Travel, for example, is a partnership with Travelocity. As with Amazon, it took hundreds of millions of dollars to build the Yahoo! technology and relationship platform, but Yahoo! now has as broad a range of cost options as any firm could enjoy. There is minimal incentive for it to add fixed costs or own and operate any of the services that it offers. Its 2003 financial report shows this cost optionality, outlined in Table 7.3.

Table 7.3   Yahoo!'s Financials[5] (billions of dollars)

	2001	2002	2003
Revenues	0.7	1.0	1.6
Cost of goods	0.2	0.2	0.4
Net operating income	−0.1	0.1	0.3
Inventory	0.0	0.0	0.0
Plant and equipment	0.1	0.4	0.4

Yahoo!'s ability to scale via components is shown by comparing its revenue growth to its fixed-asset and operating-cost growth. This is also the opportunity of the pure online player: a cost structure that is fundamentally variable and that thus leverages flexibility and margins. Yahoo! pays only for what it uses, and component owners typically pay Yahoo! a commission to add their components to its platform.

Such a cost structure may not be well suited to other companies, however. Wal-Mart, for instance, needs stores and facilities, about $52 billion of assets, along with its inventories, which adds another $25 billion, and the labor costs of more than 1 million employees. Its cost of sales is $191 *billion* on sales of $244 billion. Wal-Mart is moving in the same direction as Yahoo!, though, because it is using its platform to componentize the supply chain and move to a variable-cost structure. Vendor-managed inventory (VMI) is an example of a component that is coordinated through Wal-Mart's platform on a cost basis. Wal-Mart does not "buy" the goods; the supplier stocks the shelf, and Wal-Mart pays when the goods are sold. Its VMI partnership with P&G transformed their supplier/retailer relationship from control based to collaboration. P&G stocks the shelves and forecasts future sales trends on the basis of componentized links to Wal-Mart's in-store point-of-sale data. Wal-Mart carries no costs of inventory for the product.

More and more companies are turning expensive fixed costs into variable costs and improving quality at the same time through what we call an incremental evolution rather than a radical revolution. Many of the examples discussed in earlier chapters have moved manufacturing from in-house to component sourcing. Commodity back-office processes that add no value for the company but tie up capital and add to overhead are being outsourced: Call centers, document processing, and HR administration are leading examples.

Why Shift the Costs When You Can Avoid Them?

The Internet is a proven vehicle for turning a company's administra-tive back-office cost into the customer's valued front office. Self-management gives customers convenience, control, and flexibility in handling their relationships with a company, and the company can immediately move overhead into variable costs. Hundreds of instances of just this transformation have made the web an integral organizational-process coordination channel as well as online customer service channel. Here's just one: 80 percent of the 60 million phone calls Wells Fargo received each year were for account balance information, at a per call cost of around $10. Self-service via the web drops this cost to 10 cents or less per call. If Wells Fargo hadn't been able to recognize the inherent value of componentizing its customer service, it could well have chosen to outsource its call center overseas, cutting cost by a percentage but never leveraging its architecture to grow.

Much of this customer self-management avoids costs rather than cuts costs. FedEx estimates that it avoided adding more than 600 customer service reps through its web site self-management business componentization.[6] Customer, employee, and vendor self-service helped IBM avoid more than $5 billion in expenses. IBM simply put customer service, procurement, and e-learning online and reduced the duplicate offline processes. This cost avoidance is a growth enhancer because the increase in revenues does not produce a comparable increase in cost or overhead.

> *Every well-managed growth-platform firm makes cost avoidance a priority.*

One distinctive feature of companies that componentize their business is that they aggressively push commoditization. They exploit their cost edge not to increase but to *cut* prices, to reduce margin for component suppliers, not platform players. Amazon cut the price of best-selling books by 50 percent at a time when it was still a long way from making profits;[7] this shot across the metaphorical bow of Barnes & Noble was a bet on Amazon's growth platform. Amazon has also absorbed expensive shipping costs as a "free" incentive to customers, but its cost structures mean that it can afford these reductions in margin while its competitors cannot.

In the commodity PC space, Dell has exploited its platform capabilities to drive down prices. On one occasion, when ex-HP Chairman Carly Fiorina announced that earnings would fall below forecast because of industry price cutting, Dell slashed personal computer prices by 22 percent the very next day.[8] It could afford to do so because of its cost structures; it has an overhead of only 9 percent and, because of its direct model and platform capabilities, holds only four days of inventory. Its low overhead is a direct result of its highly componentized supply chain and innovations in process rather than product innovation.

Overhead is now the main controllable cost of a business. In the old control economy, raw materials and labor typically amounted to about 85 percent of costs, and overhead was what was left over. In commoditized ecosystems, such as auto parts, consumer electronics, and consumer loans, prices are normalized, and if one player cuts prices, the rest have little choice but to follow. Global sourcing then logically becomes the norm, because componentization and labor costs drop. As this process continues, overhead becomes the main differentiator of financial performance, a frightening situation for any old-guard firm.

Overhead is cost that adds nothing to performance. Its only value is negative; when administrative functions fail, they cause disruptions, and when they are handled well, customers get billed, HR flows smoothly, and travel expenses get paid promptly. That's it. The obvious solution is to componentize them and shrink the controllable-cost base. GE componentized internal back-office processes. IBM, Sun Microsystems, FedEx, Cisco, Wells Fargo, and Southwest componentize customer ordering and support. Supply chain management and logistics leaders synchronize complex relationships via standard interfaces. Fortune 1,000 firms componentize processes via their technology platforms and outsource call centers and HR administration.

Overhead is also the edge for platform-based electronic component suppliers. Their clients operate with 16 percent to 20 percent overhead levels, but they can focus their own operations very narrowly and operate with just 3 percent to 5 percent overhead. This is achieved through the opposite change: High fixed costs give them economies of scale but rigidity in the range of services that they provide.

Leveraging Components, Even if They Aren't Your Own

FedEx was "dismissed as an also-ran to UPS" not long ago, and to Wall Street, it looked as if FedEx was doomed to years of shrinking revenues and falling margins. Some analysts even went so far as to say "FedEx would disappear in a takeover."[9] The analysts were wrong, and FedEx has come back by building a bang-up ground network. Its resurgence came from the surprising growth of a ground-delivery service that FedEx "cobbled together" from acquisitions and the use of independent trucking firms.

This shouldn't be surprising to anyone who knows FedEx's history, because FedEx has always been a platform-driven company. It didn't cobble *anything* together but integrated new business components into its platform.

FedEx's expansion of its ground operations required no restructuring. The only restructuring costs were for early-retirement and severance programs in its mature core Express business.

Chairman and founder Fred Smith explains that "there is no other restructuring required, in our opinion, to achieve our margin goals."[10] The aggressive expansion that included acquisitions was not a disruption to the organization or a new stress for the culture; it was an enhancement of capabilities.

One analyst highlights the platform payoff for FedEx: "The key decision for FedEx was to resist building a system from scratch."[11] Instead, in 1998, it purchased Caliber Systems, owner of Roadway Package System, Roberts Express, Viking Freight, and some regional trucking companies. FedEx also hired independent truckers, operating out of 27 regional hubs, to build FedEx Ground from scratch. FedEx reported that its total investment in freight and ground over the five years (1998–2002) was $3 billion. The truckers immediately benefited from the FedEx technology and process base with scheduling and coordination, and the hubs have long been at the leading edge of automation: Packages that enter are automatically routed through the delivery-management system, and FedEx is in the freight and ground-delivery package business for what looks like a very reasonable investment.

Technology is a core part of the FedEx platform and has been since 1979, when the COSMOS global tracking system was introduced. In the 1980s, FedEx gave 100,000 PCs to large customers, enabling them to self-manage their transactions and accounts. In 1986, it launched SuperTracker, a hand-held barcode scanner to capture package information, and three years later launched its on-board satellite-based communication system to track vehicles. FedEx was a very early adopter of the Web, providing package tracking for all customers. (UPS was introducing its own innovations, too.) By 1998, FedEx was spending 1 billion a year on its technology/process infrastructure, on revenues of $10 billion.

FedEx Ground meant a sharp turn away from its Express strategy. A key element had always been its exploitation of airline deregulation of larger freight planes. While its competitors bought space on airline carriers' planes—a variable cost—FedEx built its own airline—a largely fixed cost—of more than 600 planes. FedEx used the very same platform in its Express services to ensure the same level of quality with Ground and its own cost efficiency but with far more cost optionality; the independent truckers work under incentive-based long-term contracts.

Growth platforms are far more than technology. FedEx's platform, like that of Southwest Airlines, was built on governance rules for mobilizing and rewarding people and for ensuring that they take responsibility and follow the corporate way. One of FedEx's few missteps came in the late 1970s, when it acquired a British company during a down period in the UK economy, acquiring a largely unionized labor force strongly opposed to change. FedEx had built a strong set of governance principles and organizational practices that had led to a highly disciplined and motivated culture, but this organizational platform did not transfer to the UK firm. After rebuilding, FedEx's UK operation is a leader, not a laggard, in Europe, and FedEx's platform reaches out effectively across all of Europe.

In 2003, FedEx extended its platform by purchasing Kinko's for $2.2 billion. A thriving business, Kinko's offers many opportunities for FedEx to grow, including the increased shipping services for the many small businesses that use Kinko's as their offices and the many added extra pick-up points. How about storing spare parts for FedEx logistics service customers? The Kinko's locations are in major cities, near business complexes, and are now miniwarehouses that FedEx can use to pick up and deliver parts. Same platform, extended value web.

The competition between FedEx and UPS has been to the benefit of customers and has played a major role in the reshaping of business logistics. Their platforms are their strategy. In many instances, they are so integral to customers' operations that they are now part of their customers' platforms'. That is what collaborative value webs are all about.

The Fixed-Cost Burden

Companies that have a largely variable-cost structure can adjust volumes quickly and easily. They add or reduce costs as they go, and their restructuring charges are low and infrequent. Fixed costs, on the other hand, do not go away so simply. It is sensible for companies to dispose of old facilities when they can replace them with new ones, but is it logical to do the same with people or assets that are not critical to the success of the business and that others can provide on a variable-cost basis?

Shifting to a variable cost, cosourcing structure helps mitigate these problems. When restructuring charges are a recurring item on the income statement, it is time to rethink cost structures. The platform edge comes from having more options. We do not suggest that companies move to a variable-cost environment as a matter of routine, but we do argue that a fixed-cost structure that results in restructuring charge after restructuring charge is surely not well suited to a changing environment.

Restructuring charges are often huge. One major manufacturer reported operating profit in the third quarter of 2003 of $866 million but also reported restructuring charges of $501 million: 60 percent of profits. In its annual report, the firm further warns that its inability to implement its planned reorganization may cause it to have insufficient financial resources to carry out research and development. The firm also cites regional labor regulations and union contracts that may make it impossible to implement such reorganizations. Its industry was busy commoditizing while it is trapped in the death spiral of commodity hell. The result: low utilization ratios at manufacturing facilities and higher ratios of fixed costs to sales.

Companies can exploit the componentization and platform capabilities to avoid getting stuck with restructuring as a cost of doing business. Another large corporation's annual report explains its $700 million, three-year restructuring costs this way: "Reduced full-time equivalent employees.... Consolidation of 33 domestic branch offices.... The removal of certain hardware, software, and equipment.... Withdrawal from certain international operations.... Sublease excess facilities.... Reduction in administration office space.... Write-downs of fixed assets.... Initial restructuring charges in a 2001 Workforce reduction of $182 million, Facilities reduction of $139 million, Systems removal costing $61 million." Nowhere does it note that all these costs might have been avoided through a variable-cost structure.

Finding the Balance Point Between Fixed and Variable Costs

IBM's Global Services organization has developed a useful way of thinking about the optimal cost structure for a firm. The logic is based on the observation that a firm can be fairly sure of some subset of its projected revenues for the coming years.

Here is a hypothetical example for a firm we will call XYZ. Its business plan aims for revenues of $2.3 billion, of which $1.8 billion of this is fairly certain. XYZ aims to optimize its cost structures to meet this level of sales, focusing on in-house resources. The next $0.3 billion is probable, the remaining $0.2 billion is more uncertain, and there is a possibility that sales could surge if the economy improves and new-product introductions are successful. XYZ's planning process relies on handling the risk elements of the plan through variable-cost cosourcing and value web relationships. The calculations are complex, but the logic is clear: Hedge your risks and ensure your efficiency through cost optionality.

XYZ develops cost-structure options, assuming that the business plan will turn out to be on target. The high-fixed-cost plan allows the firm to exploit scale and efficiency, but it loses flexibility and adds substantial risks if the $2.3 billion of revenues do not occur; XYZ then has an exposure of $500 million. That exposure is reduced by increasing the use of variable-cost sourcing.

The two extremes in the model are fixed costs and variable costs. Each has advantages and disadvantages that depend mostly on the predictability of market demand. Together, they help define a "balance point" in the optimization of cost structures.

> *Environmental uncertainty favors variable-cost structures.*

The balance point is essentially risk hedging: distinguishing stable ongoing business, predictable extension business, and uncertain, at-risk business. The strategic question for any firm is always how to fund the risk growth. For ongoing business, it makes sense to use the firm's platform aggressively to attack overhead and reduce working capital via sourcing of component capabilities. Many fixed costs will remain in place and provide the company with its coordination base and platform foundations, but the result will be a cost-efficient company, bullet proofed against commoditization.

Growth comes from expanding risk areas, however. This is where a company needs cost flexibility to ensure business flexibility. There are a number of factors to trade off against one another: investment cost and time, scaling volumes up or down in response to customer demand, and organizational costs of cultural adaptation, new skills, and administrative additions.

No one can provide a reliable and foolproof way of handling growth risk; otherwise, it wouldn't be risk, but this key area of business innovation can be handled through platform collaborations and made as much variable cost as is practical.

Each type of growth platform that we discussed in Chapter 6, "Expand Your Growth Space," pushes business more and more toward variable costs rather than fixed costs, but this is not an absolute. There will always be good reason for firms to keep some operations in-house and invest in fixed and intangible assets.

Letting go of fixed assets will help your business grow.

Summary

Growth should never come at the expense of profits, and in a commoditized world, cost, not revenue, is the generator of profit. At the same time, growth never comes from cutting costs alone, at least not in a long-term, sustainable manner. The solution is to change your cost structures, to build a business platform that enables you to find the optimal balance between fixed and variable costs, along with sufficient componentization to allow you to outsource or retain in-house, based on the best expected results for your business.

8

FROM VISION TO RESULTS: THE LEADERSHIP AGENDA

Leadership is often confused with personality and management style. Many business books—and executive memoirs—adopt a Hollywood model of the leader as charismatic hero, flamboyant communicator, brave lone ranger, and fierce warrior. It's Gary Cooper as the marshall standing alone against the outlaws in *High Noon*. But that metaphor presumes that you think that leadership is about killing the competition. Such leaders fight battles and then disappear into the sunset, their job done. If only it were so simple and so exciting!

What *Is* Leadership?

Business leadership includes personality and style, but great business leaders are also measured by their credibility, communication, and commitment to a mission. What differentiates great business leaders is their ability to see the future and create a path from here to there.

The word that crops up again and again in business books is "reality": identifying the business-growth path, starting the journey, and providing maps and supplies to the team. As writer Noel Tichy states:[1]

> Leaders stage revolutions. They (1) see reality: size up the situation as it really is, and (2) mobilize the appropriate resources. That is a lot harder than it sounds. Seeing reality means removing the filters that screen out the things they might not want to see, acknowledge their own and their companies' shortcomings, and accept the need to change.

Tichy observes that company founders often see realities better than their competitors do: Fred Smith saw the new reality of massive demand for package shipments in the emerging global marketplace. Competitors fretted about the difficulties and cost of updating existing delivery platforms; Smith built a unique new platform with Federal Express. Sam Walton anticipated the shift of retailing from department stores and low-quality discount stores to localized outlets in rural settings and created Wal-Mart. Herb Kelleher saw the opportunity to challenge the expensive airline hub strategy and radically cut both costs and prices by using a different strategy, leading Southwest Airlines to explosive growth. We would say that these leaders all had a sense of their new "reality" and did something about it.

Leadership is all about seeing and defining reality. The linked forces of competitive intensity, business componentization, and value webs are the way the world is moving—and moving very quickly. Yet less than 10 percent of company executives see this reality when they view their business landscapes. For many senior and middle managers, the ideas of components, platforms, value webs, and enterprise productivity are not at all obvious and conflict with their own experiences and roles in the organization.

If this is the coming reality—and we certainly think it is—someone right at the top of the organization has to get the message out and set a corporate direction for responding to, instead of ignoring or avoiding, reality. Leaders translate their vision, whether as the environmental forces of competitive intensity, the opportunity of growth platforms, or a unique vision of new modes of business, into organizational vision, governance, and mobilization.

In a nutshell, leaders make reality for the business.

Making the Right Leadership Moves

In previous chapters, we focused on the *why* and *what* of letting go to grow: the ecosystem drivers, the platform imperative, and the new value webs of modern business. Now let's spend some time exploring the all-important *how*: how to reinvent your company as an innovative growth business regardless of where your firm is now positioned.

There are two key leadership roles: The first is to articulate the vision of the company—the "why change." The second is to link that vision to execution through management, measurement, and governance systems that create highly visible recognition and reward for those who model the new behaviors.

- **Articulate the vision**—Leaders must articulate both the vision and the need for change. That vision must be clear, consistent, and repeatable, and leaders must provide visible support for change—communicating consistently and often and listening always. This sends a clear signal to the business that through governance, platform architectures, and accelerated local initiatives, the change becomes obvious. Leadership means intervening in what Jack Welch calls the "social architecture" of the firm; it interrupts business as usual with business unusual.

> *Let's repeat that: Interrupt business as usual with business unusual.*

- **Link vision to execution**—The policies, principles, mandates, and enablers that provide the frameworks for taking the initiative to all levels of the organization are critical. Call this the management system, the governance model, or the "big rules," if you want. But big rules must be accompanied by cross-organizational improvements, execution, and reward and recognition systems that overtly reinforce the desired change.

Leadership no longer means command and control. It no longer means "my values" but rather shared values. It means collaboration, empowerment, and the ability to enable decision making in the business—any business—to occur closer to the customer. Although the leader's vision can be delivered vertically, it will drive growth only if it is accepted and implemented horizontally, across the organization.

Articulating the Vision Through Shared Values

IBM does business in more than 170 countries worldwide and faces some uniquely modern challenges: 40 percent of its workforce is mobile, and more then half of its staff has been employed at IBM for less than five years.

Sam Palmisano recognized that a major change was approaching in the IT industry when he accepted the CEO position in 2002. The industry was splitting into two growth areas: low-cost, undifferentiated products and high-value integration based on innovation and focused on a complete transformation of the enterprise.

For commodity suppliers, growth would come from a stripped-down business model that valued speed and ceaselessly lowered cost. For enterprise providers, growth would come through innovation, client intimacy, and integrated solutions. IBM chose the enterprise space, focused on the idea that the company was at its best when creating value that clients could not get from anyone else. To succeed in this space required a dedication to leading-edge technology, services, expertise, and intellectual capital and the integration of those capabilities to provide a competitive advantage to customers. By focusing on the value-add space, IBM generates superior returns when compared to the overall IT industry and commands a leadership position in its selected businesses.

For Palmisano, leadership execution meant letting go of historical corporate beliefs and driving the creation of a new set of company values that position IBM as a leader in this new industry space. He saw the new reality for IBM, but the task was to communicate this vision across the business.

In July 2003, Palmisano opened up IBM's corporate intranet to a companywide "jam," a discussion of IBM's values. Palmisano didn't create a task force, didn't ask his senior management team to produce a set of recommendations, and didn't hire an outside business guru. Instead, to ensure relevance, credibility, and acceptance, he went directly to IBM's 320,000 employees and asked *them* to identify what they thought IBM's values should be.

All IBM employees were invited to examine their relationship with the company and with one another. The discussion raged online over four days, ranging from direct criticism to constructive debate, and the employees gradually shaped and committed to three values that define and guide the company into the future:

- Dedication to every client's success

- Innovation that matters—for IBM and for the world

- Trust and personal responsibility in all relationships

"You had to put your ego aside—not an easy thing for a CEO to do—and realize that this was the best thing that could have happened," said Palmisano. "You could say, 'I've unleashed this incredible negative energy.' Or you could say, 'I now have this incredible mandate to drive even more change in the company.'"

"How do you channel this diverse and constantly changing array of talent and experience into a common purpose? How do you get people to passionately pursue that purpose?" asks Palmisano. "You could employ all kinds of traditional management processes. But they wouldn't work at IBM—or, I would argue, at an increasing number of twenty-first century companies. You can't impose command-and-control mechanisms on a large, highly professional workforce. The CEO can't say to them, 'Get in line and follow me.' Or 'I've decided what your values are.' You lay out the opportunity to become a great company again—the greatest in the world. And you hope people feel the same need, the urgency you do, to get there. I think IBMers today do feel that urgency. Maybe the jam's greatest contribution was to make that fact unambiguously clear to all of us, very visibly, in public."[2]

This IBM "jam" led directly to a new set of management systems and rewards that include employee ideas and are driving visible change in how IBM works both with clients and internally. Fundamental policies have been changed within the organization, including driving pricing decisions closer to the client. IBM's fast-growing services teams are now refocused on *client satisfaction with their solutions*, not solely on how many deals the team closes, encouraging client intimacy over aggressive sales efforts.

To retain its leadership position in the technology industry and ensure that it is a critical component of its value webs, IBM faces the same challenge that many other firms must wrestle with: letting go of unhealthy, unproductive elements of corporate culture to allow the firm to grow.

Leadership is about listening, about letting go of control and creating a shared sense of collaboration for the greater good of the firm.

Execution Through Collaboration

Culture is the primary issue discussed in strategy meetings, whether they're the largest enterprise in the world or the smallest. The questions are always the same, too: How do we change our entrenched culture? How do we drive change that will enable a competitive edge, get us to market more quickly, or develop deeper relationships with our clients and teammates?

Collaboration is the competitive edge. All the major business movements of the past decade have sought to foster collaboration, but the reality of too many organizations is still built around a command-and-control management structure with carefully guarded territory and information, hidden internal competition, and limited coordination ability. There is plenty of coordination built upon communication—the transmitting of information—but very few business components based on collaboration, the act of shared *creation and discovery.*

The challenge is that to see maximal value, creation and collaboration must go together. In the arts, sciences, sports, government, politics, and business, everyday innovation rests on collaboration.

Collaboration is a difficult skill to foster at the personal level and even more difficult to promote and encourage as the focus expands to groups, business units, the enterprise, and the full range of value webs. Further, collaboration is not a wishy-washy search for agreement but a tough-minded process, resting on trust in one another's reliability and commitment. Good intentions are not enough; your teams need to have the confidence that they can count on one another. It demands argument and, yes, creative conflict. It demands that someone take the risk and call the meeting. Collaboration also demands that leaders not only model but also reward this behavior.

As the innovation economy flourishes, companies are moving from value derived from assets to value based on the knowledge of its people. Industrial Age thinking about culture simply does not cut it in the post–Industrial Age.

Teams and individuals must openly combine knowledge, experience, and expertise: It is this alchemy that drives breakthrough innovation.

The effects of collaboration are even more dramatic when individuals, teams, and even enterprises work outside of their own business areas. Most organizations know how to collaborate in an emergency, in a crisis. They do it instinctively because they know that crisis collaboration is imperative for the survival of the business. However, it's the ad hoc, everyday collaboration that needs to be fostered and rewarded to ensure the long-term growth of the business. The ability of leaders to infuse collaboration into the business will have a dramatic effect on the rate and pace at which the organization transforms itself. Indeed, the level of collaboration will end up as either an accelerator or a decelerator of growth.

The most famous scientific and artistic partnerships, such as James Watson and Francis Crick or John Lennon and Paul McCartney, were always on the edge of hostility; they collaborated because they knew that they would produce better results together than by working separately.

Collaborators often have differing interests. Companies that are growth leaders in collaborative supply chain management are still buyers and sellers looking to maximize their own operations. Within companies, people have a legitimate concern that collaboration may put their own jobs at risk. But there's no way to stop the tide: The more that collaboration centers on innovation, the more that collaborators must share their intellectual capital.

Because collaboration is so difficult to build and institutionalize, so intimately linked to creativity, and so central to the relationship building needed for value web expansion, it is a firm's competitive edge in the Innovation Economy. The commoditization cycle will invariably drive you away from collaboration, because a commodity marketplace is intensely transaction-focused—a buyer/seller competition. We cannot emphasize enough the necessity of your search for this competitive edge. All leading companies will put this theory to use, not simply memorialize it in their vision and values statements.

Leadership in Action

To illustrate leadership in action, let's revisit General Electric, Procter & Gamble, and Amazon to consider the role of leadership in their growth strategies. In each instance, we'll explain how the link from idea to action occurred via the leader's championing change and the implementation of new, relevant big rules and governance.

General Electric

The classic big rule was the one stated by CEO Jack Welch in 1981: "Fix, Sell, or Close." An excellent leader, he used this rule to champion his vision of GE being either number one or two in a market or withdrawing. The famous three-circle chart shown in Figure 8.1 captures this thinking. "Any business outside the circles, I told [my wife] Caroline, we would fix, sell, or close."[3]

Figure 8.1 Jack Welch's vision for a new GE.

In the late 1980s, Jack Welch began to work on the social architecture of GE because "a company can boost productivity by restructuring, removing bureaucracy, and downsizing, but cannot sustain high productivity without cultural change." Speed, simplicity, and self-confidence were the core elements of the new GE.

Between 1989 and 1992, GE launched three cultural initiatives called Work Out, Boundaryless Company, and Stretch Goals. By working on the social architecture, Welch was able to transform the inherently dynamic process of governance.

Between 1987 and 1999, Jack also championed services, globalization, Six Sigma, and e-business initiatives. These were launched into the GE "operating system," an annual cycle whereby new ideas are introduced and allocated resources, executive focus, key metrics, and reviews throughout the year.

The e-business initiative spawned GE's current move toward componentization. In working to fulfill Welch's vision of buying and selling online, GE business units quickly recognized the value of simplifying the back-office processes, which directly stimulated today's efforts to simplify, centralize, and create common back-office processes across their enterprise.

Procter & Gamble

CEO A. G. Lafley's stated vision is that Procter & Gamble will do only what it does best and that half of all new products should originate outside P&G. As he explained, "innovation and discovery are likely to come from anywhere. What P&G is really good at is developing innovations and commercializing them. So what I said is, 'We need an open marketplace.' We're probably as good as the next guy at inventing. But we are not absolutely and positively better than everybody else at inventing."[4]

Lafley's plan for outsourcing is simply that if it is not a core competence, the new P&G won't do it. P&G has now outsourced Ivory soap manufacturing, IT operations, and HR administration. A. G. Lafley is championing change in a dramatic way, with both the corporate vision and the big rules. Requiring that half of all new products originate outside the firm is very much the type of strategic change we are evangelizing herein.

But change isn't about steamrolling over existing culture either. Lafley's goal is to preserve "the core of the culture and pull people where I wanted to go. I enrolled them in change. I didn't tell them."[5]

Amazon.com

CEO Jeff Bezos has led Amazon into a commoditized market through a compelling picture of a practical, attractive, and profitable future. His guiding principles are that customers will be able to find, discover, and buy *anything* online and that Amazon will be the most customer-centric company online. That principle is very different from stating that customers will be able to buy anything online, that customers will be able to buy anything stored in our distribution centers, or that Amazon will always have the lowest prices.

Bezos expanded on what he believes is required to become the most customer-centric online player:[6]

> Three things: listen, invent, and personalize. Listen to what customers want, and figure out how to give it to them. The second thing we do is invent for customers, because it's not the customer's job to invent for themselves. The third thing is to personalize. This is the newest part of customer at the center. And we're talking about putting each customer at the center of his/her universe. If we have 17 million customers, we should have 17 million stores.

Many of Amazon's innovations emerge from the deceptively simple mantra of listen, invent, personalize. One example is One-Click, its highly componentized technology platform built *entirely* on open standards and interfaces.

Bezos's guiding principles continue to lead the company's strategic direction with market prioritization, geographic expansion, and organizational and technical architecture. They are the basis for such big rules as the Amazon mandate that all processes must have "clean" interfaces. They also enable the componentization of alliances: "We won't use our digital business platform to build the Earth's most customer-centric company alone—we'll do it with thousands of partners of all sizes."[7]

Today, the interplay among vision, big rules, governance, initiatives, and enterprise productivity is much more iterative. In January 2000, the executive team made the decision to display goods sold by all Amazon sellers in a completely integrated fashion. They called this concept a "single store" and neatly integrated its componentization process for the customer.

The introduction of free shipping on all purchases over a certain amount was another important initiative. Amazon's own metrics on growth and margins made it clear that lowering prices and all associated costs were key to continuous profitable growth. This led Amazon's continuous drive for efficiency as a critical component of growth innovation. Amazon's leadership-empowerment strategy integrates its vision, rules, and metrics and sets the stage for Amazon's internal governance and business structure. Just as important, this concept was not part of Bezos's initial vision but the result of well-coordinated, open communications up and down the management hierarchy.

Amazon would not have moved along the path to being highly componentized without its leadership principles, and it could not have done so without a platform that coordinates so many technical, business, and organizational components.

> Developing good business direction is not magic; it's a tough and sometimes exhausting process of gathering and analyzing information. Many of the best visions are not brilliantly innovative but have an almost mundane quality, often consisting of *ideas* that are already well known.[8]

We add this thought: The leader spots the direction the world is moving in, locates an opportunity for the firm, and creates the new reality for the organization. It is mundane, in the sense of "down to earth, relating to reality."

Summary

The best corporate restructuring in the world won't matter unless there's leadership from the executive team and a clear message being sent to the management and staff that these changes are critical to the long-term health and survival of the company. Leadership is about seeing and, yes, *defining* reality, for both the company and the shareholders. That's why we believe that there are two key leadership roles: articulating the vision and linking vision to execution by ensuring that your personal actions and companywide rewards encourage desired behaviors and efforts by your team.

9

ACHIEVING MEASURABLE PRODUCTIVITY IMPROVEMENTS

O ne of the most common failings with business books is that they all present new frameworks, offer different philosophies for your company, and even suggest specific strategies for your type of business, but they *never explain how to implement the change.* We're presenting a radical reinvention of your business in this book too, because we're absolutely convinced that if you don't let go, you cannot grow in this new century.

The question is how to achieve these changes, how to recognize that you're in a commoditized business space—or one in which commoditization is looming just beyond the visible horizon—and how to transform your company into a growth organization.

The first step toward implementation is quantification, and this chapter is about identifying the measures of productivity that will help you lead *your* company through this transition. But first things first. Let's talk about productivity and how to measure it so that you'll be able to ensure that you are moving on the path toward componentization, not the road to commodity hell.

Measuring Productivity

Ever-increasing productivity is the goal for all facets of every business. It is, alas, also one of the most elusive concepts in economics and one of the most difficult for businesses to define and measure, for both tracking their performance and rewarding their employees.

"Productivity," per se, is an invention of the Industrial Revolution. The most frequent embodiment of productivity is to gauge the efficient use of existing resources: a manufacturing concept of productivity.

As post–Industrial Age companies evolve from businesses based on hard assets to businesses based on people, productivity needs to change too, to allow better measure of the productivity *of people*.

Why productivity? Because increased productivity is what allows companies to pay performance bonuses, raise pay, and fuel long-term sustainability through acquisitions and investments in high-growth areas and new markets. It's also a major factor in a company's earnings per share growth, a key measure of corporate performance. The creation of a more scientific approach to measuring people productivity is crucial.

Let's boil it down to its essence, though, so we can rebuild the concept of productivity measurement as a strategic asset for any company. All measures of productivity are a ratio: outputs over inputs. The question is *which* outputs and *which* inputs to measure. The traditional efficiency model measures physical outputs divided by physical inputs. Typical examples are manufacturing oriented—for example, the number of consumer appliances or electronics or the number of cars rolling off the assembly line per day/week/month/year. Both outputs are measured against the input (head count) expended to deliver the output.

But are those the right measures?

Measuring the Right Factors to Encourage Growth

As said previously, productivity is a ratio. But sustained organic growth through productivity can be achieved only by *linking* the numerator and the denominator—whatever they may be—to your business. The challenge within most organizations today is that instead of promoting the necessity of increasing the numerator (revenue, profit, gross margin), companies have become expert at driving down the denominator (expense, headcount, SG&A) in the game of reduction. Consider the core philosophies underlying supply chain management or production and administrative-process reengineering. These philosophies have been a natural organizational response to the volatility of the marketplace in the post-dot-com collapse, but they aren't *growth* drivers.

> *Sustained organic growth through productivity can be achieved only by linking the numerator and the denominator.*

Companies have become skilled at driving efficiency through the overwhelming and sustained success of such initiatives as Six Sigma. Driving efficiency is not equal to driving growth, however. There needs to be an equal focus on growth through a balanced relationship based on efficiency (denominator) *plus* growth (numerator) enabled by productivity, collaboration, and innovation. Growth comes when process, people, and technology are integrated and working in concert so the firm can focus on delivering innovation and differentiation for the client. This is what clients value most and are willing to pay a premium for.

Many companies have experienced periods during which labor costs increase more quickly than revenue. A fanatical devotion to taming and ultimately reducing labor costs, however, is myopic and has negative consequences for the long-term growth of the company. One point we like to make is that *you cannot cut yourself to revenue growth. The denominator can go no lower than zero, but the numerator is infinite.*

Companies have also learned that investment in their brands, relationships, and client-satisfaction processes can put more staying power behind that growth (though not always, as bookstores have learned as they've struggled with the question of how to compete with Amazon and other pure component players).

Change the driver to innovation, and it becomes clear that companies are less skilled at driving either of the two components of the productivity equation, let alone both. Yet it is innovation that is key in times of rapid change and market discontinuities, innovation that cannot be accomplished through these same operational factors or the existing company culture. It demands a nimble culture comfortable with change, evolution, collaboration, and letting go. Just as important from a leadership perspective, it also demands that the rest of the organization be given clear and consistent signals about what leadership expects and how incentives and rewards will be calculated.

There must be a constant and consistent approach to balanced focus on and measurement of continuous profitable growth through productivity, collaboration, and innovation, not only volume. Productivity, collaboration, and innovation are the top-line growth drivers, the sister algorithm to Six Sigma, with all it did for driving organizational efficiency and bottom-line cost savings.

It is in this fusion of the opposing forces of efficiency and growth where our Let Go to Grow philosophy really shines, where it becomes clear that the whole really is greater than the sum of the parts.

Growth requires *productivity* across the enterprise, through processes and tools that free up time via componentization and new process and service designs, and *collaboration* across relationships and across lines of business. The result is *innovation* that builds new value webs and extends the firm's value space. Productivity, collaboration, and innovation are thus intrinsically linked. If they are not, dysfunctional reward systems will stymie efforts to improve productivity, and the dysfunctional climate of an efficiency-focused business will block collaboration.

Productivity as a Growth Strategy

An *efficiency culture* keeps the organization on a path that ensures that the firm maintains control. It lowers the denominator in very controlled and measurable ways but doesn't emphasize increasing the numerator or growing the business.

A *growth culture*, by contrast, takes *action*. A growth culture is one in which people make decisions lower in the organizational hierarchy, take initiatives, earn personal rewards, and create a sense of accomplishment. This growth-oriented culture views efficiency as a tangent or even a roadblock to innovation.

Neither culture creates both growth and profits, though, so the obvious question is: Can these two cultures of growth and efficiency be merged, with the goal of continuous profitable growth? The answer we offer is yes, but only if your productivity measures help propel your firm toward growth and only if your corporate culture supports the changes and reinvention that will inevitably be required.

A firm's culture is shaped by many factors, including history, personal characteristics, individual and organizational values, trust, incentive and reward systems, organizational structures, skills, attitudes, professional training, experience, and demographics. Some cultures are simply not geared to collaborative action, and in many firms, the corporate culture reinforces established fiefdoms and isolation from "outsiders." Researchers refer to this as NIH, or *not invented here* syndrome, whereby companies waste thousands of hours creating something that is more efficiently purchased or licensed from a third party.

Some cultures are also consensual and conservative, causing many actions that are key to corporate growth to be blocked or delayed for months, or even years. Welcoming diversity and risk is key to creativity and productivity. Let go of yesterday; let go of control.

It can be phenomenally difficult to change a corporate culture. Business history is littered with outsider CEOs who tried to force corporate change, just to have the entire company collapse and die. There are actions that can be taken to shape these cultures, however, that create greater agility and drive enterprise productivity and continuous profitable growth. In every growth leader we have studied, we find an almost obsessive focus on efficiency and costs. The growth leaders have a simultaneous expansive and energetic commitment to "more" and "new"—innovation, services, markets, and value web relationships—balanced with great attention paid to efficiency and cost. By contrast, the dot-com era was characterized by an exclusive focus on the new, without ever paying attention to costs, efficiency, and profitability.

Innovation, service, relationships, and collaboration—the engines of profitable growth—do not lead to meaningful quantification of relative performance, though. In fact, we've come full circle. In particular, collaboration is difficult to energize, because individual effort is the cornerstone of company incentive systems, and both budgeting and financial performance measurement end up as obstacles on the way to a collaborative culture. Every leadership team wrestles with the question of how to ensure and encourage collaboration.

And collaboration will increasingly play a larger part both in individual skills and as a macro business issue. Look at the explosion of blogs in the past few years, the emergence of social networking, of wikis. Just as the PC changed the workforce and how we collaborated in the 1980s and 1990s, these new tools and ideas will change how people and teams work together over the next ten years. It is imperative that business leaders learn how to leverage these new tools and methodologies to foster collaboration. If you don't believe us, ask your children or your grandchildren. It's those kids—the ones who are collaborating on what movie to see this weekend via a five-person instant messaging session, or adding individual ring tones to your cell phone for you—who will be entering the business world—and soon. You can choose to lead, follow, or get out of the way (we suggest you lead), but collaboration is essential to the growth equation.

If quantifiable metrics for innovation, relationships, and collaboration are difficult to create, how do the growth leaders drive enterprise productivity? By measuring productivity as the skilled use of resources.

Leadership provides the path to growth *and* efficiency—not one or the other—through componentization and effective platform deployment. Management decides which components it will own and which it will buy, focusing on internal resource capabilities, on what components of the business it can excel at, rather than simply the shallow analysis of cost savings. At IBM, we call this *economies of expertise.*

Change Your Productivity Measure, and You'll Change Your Company

The company is GE Medical Systems. The time is 1997. Jeff Immelt has just been hired as CEO and assigned the responsibility of turning around the troubled GE division, while also being groomed as a potential successor to legendary GE Chairman Jack Welch.

Immelt started by shifting the company from Maintain Control to Growth, initially through acquisitions and then through moves to componentize the business by restructuring global operations and balancing access to low-cost resources and high-end technical expertise across countries. By 2001, four years after Immelt took the helm, GE Medical Systems sales had doubled to $4 billion, and profits had increased almost threefold.[1]

Since Immelt was elevated to GE Chairman in 2001, GE's medical equipment business, now part of GE Healthcare, has continued to grow. By 2004, divisional sales had reached $10 billion. A *Forbes* article in April 2004[2] glowingly reviews its achievements, highlighting the degree to which the company has been able to maintain manufacturing jobs in the United States while still excelling in its highly componentized business segment.

A good example is GE's Waukesha (Wisconsin) plant, the production site for a $1 million computer tomography (CT) scanner that was developed by bringing top engineers from other facilities to work on site with assembly-line workers. This plant's efficiency and productivity are reflected in the 86-person cross-functional team that followed a 450-step process to produce a design that ultimately ended up involving 300 suppliers and 800 unique parts, reducing assembly safety problems by 40 percent. The team adopted lean manufacturing techniques, the obsessively efficient approach pioneered by Toyota and based on just-in-time manufacturing processes. The result: The new assembly line requires half the shop floor space of the previous-generation CT scanner and 35 percent less assembly time. Efficiency and productivity at the Waukesha plant are up 25 percent since 2001.

Business componentization changes the nature of productivity improvement and enables teams at any level of the business to make a contribution that may be entirely the opposite of ones that other units—at any level—are making. Efficiency and growth. You can address both the numerator and the denominator in the productivity equation because the business can focus in meticulous detail on improving costs, reducing time, and exploiting the very core of componentization: standardized interfaces for sourcing and deploying capabilities. This is everyday innovation—innovation as part of the culture itself, not something unusual or alien.

At the same time, the componentized business can focus its growth initiatives. The components have clean, standardized interfaces. Partners manage their own components, freeing management time to focus on what differentiates them, and drive growth. Apparel manufacturer TAL is working in an extremely commoditized ecosystem yet is a leader in several areas of high-end innovation, holding patents in making shirts wrinkle-free, for instance.

This innovation highlights two aspects of enterprise productivity: TAL has to be efficient in its highly commoditized global market and turn that commoditization to its advantage. If, for a slight premium, customers will buy shirts that are easier to iron, TAL gets a few cents extra per unit, which can add up to millions of dollars. Rather than be stuck on the lower-costs treadmill, TAL embodies the idea that innovation companies improve by increasing revenues simultaneously with careful management of labor and production costs.

Companies like TAL and GE are able to afford their investments in growth because they are efficient, and they are efficient because they grow. By focusing on productivity as a ratio, they are also productive across the enterprise and across measures of efficiency and growth, outputs over inputs.

Productivity in an Innovative World

Productivity measures remain the foundation of any business, but how do you drive and measure growth through enterprise innovation in markets, designs, technology breakthroughs, and service transformation? More important, how do you improve your productivity in a manner that's consistent with the Let Go to Grow philosophy?

The future demands people who engage in complex problem solving and contribute through creativity and collaboration. We should not measure their contribution by the time it takes to create an idea, the cost to solve a complex problem, or the volume of output. Would you measure Renoir's, Rembrandt's, or da Vinci's productivity by the denominator—the amount of paint used and hours invested—or the numerator—number of pictures produced per annum? Silly question. Yet doctors are often measured by the number of patients seen per day and academics by their volume of refereed journal articles (which makes writing a book a "nonproductive" use of time). Most people in business are measured by a comparable efficiency metric.

> *What you measure defines how people work.*

Real, sustainable growth comes from a combination of productivity and collaboration, which in turn spurs innovation, not faddish measures and metrics. Growth is not in and of itself growth *productivity*, however. The 2004 earnings report of one small company boasts of its "record revenues" of $11 million and speaks of its outstanding growth record. Given that its cost of goods was $12 million and its overhead was an additional $15 million, what was that growth really worth? The company argues that it is making the investments that will turn growth into profits, but there is absolutely no evidence for this claim. Without growth-productivity indicators, this firm remains in the "hope and a prayer" dot-com world, sustained purely by its public relations efforts and irrationally optimistic investors.

The linkages between efficiency and growth are complex, uncertain, and often contentious. In the information technology field, there has been a long-running argument about whether the billions of dollars invested in IT between the 1970s and 1990s had increased productivity, particularly in financial services. All efficiency measures show static or even declining performance.

IT proponents argued that these productivity measures did not take into account the longer time frame and greater capital investment involved in IT-based innovation; long lead times for development that reduce today's profits and efficiency in the interest of tomorrow's effectiveness; the cost of building technology platforms that enable new products, services and processes; and the organizational learning required to derive value from technology applications. R&D is comparable, too, because it is an expense to be written off that thus reduces today's efficiency in the interest of tomorrow's growth.

It's widely accepted today that long-term productivity was improved and that these infrastructure changes have enabled the growth of many industries, but none of the efficiency productivity metrics quantified this fact, and there were no convincing alternative growth metrics available to provide this evidence.

The productivity dilemma remains: How do companies ensure that they are applying resources toward profitable growth? If they impose too many inappropriate efficiency metrics, the signals that they send to the company culture produce inappropriate actions, ones that are not in the interest of either the firm or the innovators. If they do not ensure systematic measures of growth productivity, there is no basis for prioritizing investments, for monitoring projects, or for ensuring financial discipline.

If efficiency productivity metrics place too much emphasis on today at the possible—even probable—expense of the future, remember that lack of productivity measures to guide growth initiatives puts the present at risk, too. This is not a dilemma that will disappear. Enterprise productivity is created through efforts that fuse efficiency and growth, where innovation is the focus. It combines structure and innovation, efficiency and growth, and, no, these do not come together without a culture of collaboration.

A Roadmap to Improving Productivity

There are three ways to improve productivity to ensure that your firm focuses on meaningful measures and metrics and encourages a culture of revenue improvement along with cost reductions. You can, in fact, lower labor costs, optimize your workforce, and optimize your workers.

The most common approach to improving productivity is to lower labor costs through either outsourcing or global sourcing. The productivity equation factors in the cost of restructuring and the cost of subcontractors: Labor has a measurable cost whether the employee is on your payroll or the payroll of one of your componentized value web partners.

If you can't escape the cost of labor, how do you lower labor costs? This can be done through what we refer to as *workforce optimization*. Workforce optimization includes a variety of factors, from where employees sit to their level of knowledge, skills, and ability to connect with one another in this increasingly global economy. It involves the process of remixing labor in different regions and different countries to maximize revenue opportunities and minimize cost.

Global sourcing is one way to achieve this, but another, smarter way is to move the resources to where the revenue-growth opportunities are located. This is a radical idea to most organizations because most base their operations on carefully controlled plans, created on a yearly basis. They allow no strategic agility to pursue new revenue-growth opportunities, either in a new or emerging market or a hot product or service opportunity. This is frequently owing to the constraints of existing human resources or financial planning systems within large organizations, which is why collaboration—global collaboration—is so critical for long-term success. In this sense, improving productivity comes from putting your people where they can drive the most revenue for the company.

The idea behind putting your people where they can drive the most revenue—another example of workforce optimization—presupposes an enterprise view of who your people are, what skills they possess, and their availability for deployment. Human resources and financial planning organizations must invest in technologies and processes that will deliver an enterprise view to all available skills. These pools of skilled workers then allow fluid movement across the business in order to capture emerging revenue opportunities—in real time—as well as improve effectiveness and drive productivity and skills development.

Optimizing the Workforce

Worker optimization centers on the question: *How do you make a unit of labor more productive?* That is, what can you change to make someone more productive on the job? Your answer should focus on both innovative tools and process standardization, factors that allow workers to focus on high-value tasks.

One facet of worker optimization is appropriate information technology infrastructure improvements. Note that we didn't say that it's simply the inclusion of technology, however: Too many companies have been lured to their doom through the siren song of technology as the universal solution. Technology by itself won't make your workforce more productive, but it is an *enabler* of productivity improvements.

Productivity starts with freeing up employee time, which then allows employees to collaborate, to reach across divisions, sectors, and organizations to leverage the vast intellectual capital represented by the entire value web. At IBM, for example, there are 320,000 employees worldwide, and even a 10 percent increase in collaboration would produce dramatic improvements in productivity, in both the numerator and the denominator, and growth and efficiency. Indeed, cultivating this culture of collaboration is a key objective of IBM's transformation and ultimately will create the innovation that fuels its growth.

Achieving Productivity

Productivity tends to have a negative connotation: the idea that employees are going to be pushed harder to run faster and faster on the treadmill. But that's not what we're after. We're advocating automating processes, eliminating unproductive activities, streamlining decision making, and optimizing workforces and workers so that your company can react more quickly to changes in the business ecosystem and deploy resources in a much more fluid manner.

Rather than productivity being the *output* from leadership initiatives, then, it is the *input* to these initiatives. Productivity is *not* a measure of efficiency but a critical measure of how your company is letting go and growing, adapting, and evolving for the changing needs of the market as you move fully into a componentized and commoditized future.

So how can you measure the linkage between inputs and outputs? A simple example is how we have been measuring our information technology investments at IBM for the past five years. We measure the simple ratio of "transform" spend to "maintenance" spend. When we started on our path toward becoming an on demand enterprise, we were investing 12 percent of our total IT budget in transformational business initiatives. We have since driven that level of investment up to 30 percent. The investment is funded through a combination of reducing our operational expenses through traditional productivity efficiency programs and reinvesting a portion of the savings we generate from the transformational initiatives. Input is linked to output.

Another example is measuring revenue generated from your company's latest innovations. Most successful growth companies keep a close watch on how much revenue as a percentage of total revenue is generated from products and services they have released into the market over the past 12 to 24 months. If the majority of your firm's revenue is not coming from your latest innovations, you are probably on your way toward becoming commoditized. A close corollary to this is revenue concentration. If more and more of your revenue is coming from fewer and fewer clients, you are probably not linking inputs and outputs. The companies that are linked find a way to protect their base revenue yet move into new "white space" to generate growth. Keeping your pulse on revenue concentration is a good early indicator of which way your firm is headed.

Productivity metrics are a key signaling mechanism of leadership and a key listening mechanism in the organizational culture. Take a look at what signals your executive team is sending to your workforce, in terms of business case justification, capital investment planning, management development programs, incentive systems, and control systems.

Productivity rests on improving growth and efficiency with metrics that encourage cultural changes, changes that must start at the top. In the end, improving productivity is a leadership task along with a responsibility of the entire workforce.

Summary

Once your business is componentized and integrated and you have clear, engaging leadership helping the firm evolve, you should see a measurable difference in productivity. Driving both efficiency and growth in concert, through a balanced focus on productivity, collaboration, and innovation, will result in useful and comprehensible metrics to measure what's proving successful, how much it's costing the firm, and the profit it's generating. Most important, productivity metrics help you ensure that you're always improving productivity within your firm—that performance and reward systems really are producing the results sought.

10

PRACTICAL IMPLEMENTATION OF THE COMPONENT BUSINESS MODEL

T he analysis and recommendations that we have presented in the preceding chapters are derived from real-world practice, especially lessons from the companies that have set the pace for profitable growth while sustaining their competitive edge. As with any such analysis, we run the risk of making it look too easy, as if, say, the leaders of Southwest, FedEx, or Wal-Mart woke up one morning and said, "Hey, let's componentize the business! Then we can build a platform too." There is just such a sense of instant success in business books. Obviously, however, that is not the reality. Consider Toyota's legendary *kanban* system, the core of the just-in-time inventory management that underlies its lean production componentization of manufacturing, the Toyota Production System. Kanban took a decade to implement in Toyota, and TPS has evolved over a 40-year period. We'll be straight with you: Nothing that we describe in this book can be implemented instantly, and everything has an element of risk and uncertainty. There's no guarantee of success.

One advantage of hindsight is being able to identify the long-term patterns from the ups and downs of short-term uncertainty, market volatility, and the mistakes and sidetracks common to even the most exemplary firm. For our book to be of practical value, it is not enough for us to show the path to sustained profitable growth. The challenge is to help your company start off on the journey.

We offer the core principle for building profitable growth: Componentize your business. Yes, you may say, but what do we do *first*? This chapter will offer those practical answers—not *the* answer—by looking at the lessons we can learn from the pioneers in letting go to grow through componentization, platform, and value web integration.

The most obvious two characteristics of these new firms are at the extreme of long term and short term. They did not start out to componentize their businesses, but their emphasis on process and operational excellence, along with a need to find sources of differentiation in their environments, led each to focus on daily performance and efficiency productivity (the short-term extreme). Componentization then became their natural and necessary evolutionary path.

These exemplary firms have business models that embodied imperatives very early in their drive for growth—imperatives that helped guide action at all levels of the firms. Some examples are the following:

- **Cemex**—We make cement.

- **Amazon**—Customers will be able to find, discover, and buy anything online.

- **eBay**—We build community.

- **GE**—We are number 1 or 2 in every business sector we compete in, and we grow by our ability to innovate every day.

- **Dell**—We win by margins, not prices.

- **Wal-Mart**—Everyday low prices every day.

- **FedEx**—We guarantee on-time delivery.

Each of these focused strategies translates directly to process as the driver of business capabilities. That is different from the view of "process as procedure" that marks business-process reengineering, total quality management, Six Sigma, and enterprise resource planning, although these are often part of how companies create process capabilities. The exemplars' sharp operational sense of priorities moves from capabilities (How do we make cement? How do we build community?) to process (We do it this way.) to innovation (We do it better and better.). Process-driven companies—ones that define their capabilities in terms of process, not products—are thus well positioned to exploit componentization, because they have already institutionalized a culture and style of thinking that emphasize clean interfaces and appropriate standardization, both the elements of a componentized business.

These companies also show the primacy of coordination. All of them are driven by focused and clearly defined business models, as embodied by their leaders and as part of a highly coordinated policy and governance process. They have central direction, and workers are never left in doubt about top management's priorities and their own responsibilities to support them. Central coordination, though, does not mean centralized operations. The companies are not centralized in the way that head office and corporate finance were when Command and Control authority dominated so many Fortune 1,000 firms.

Such organizational centralization, which became identified with bureaucracy, is widely identified as a primary explanation for the erosion of industry leadership of so many top firms in the 1980s and 1990s. They lost flexibility because of the burden of centralization. Profitable growth companies have used standardization of processes as a vehicle to ensure consistency across the enterprise, along with local authority and accountability to foster innovation. This approach has been described as centralization-with-decentralization and the federated organization.

Coordination via standardization is common to just about every growth leader that we studied for this book. We summarize this in terms of leadership messages:

> *Demand compliance but foster innovation.*

This ethos is why these firms have been so adept in exploiting information technology as part of their process coordination and standardization. Wal-Mart and Dell helped create the supply chain management revolution that has transformed the very nature of retailing and consumer electronics. GE was among the first large companies to recognize the opportunity of Internet technology for coordinating external relationships and internal operations. Amazon and eBay went far beyond typical dot-com thinking by using the Web as the core of their customer relationship coordination and value web innovations rather than as the foundation of a shopping site. Cemex built a global reputation as a leader in the business use of IT, and information technology underlies the entire Cemex Way.

The growth leaders forged their own path by making IT core to their business and organizational capabilities. They did so at a time when the technology was not componentized but was dominated by large in-house software applications, multiple telecommunications networks, and complex, massive enterprise-processing systems. They did the best with what was available to them and frequently built atop proprietary technology that remains in use today; Wal-Mart's supply chain management systems are an example. This approach has both advantages and disadvantages—they are tailored to the organization, but other firms can catch up by utilizing the new standardized interfaces and component technology. That said, the leaders never stand still. They have their technology platform in place and are continually incorporating component technology on a selective basis. The important point is that they maintain their key enterprise-growth capability, the tight linkage between process coordination and culture, gaining productivity through efficiency and innovation.

Because they were the leaders, these firms had the time to get both process and technology right before the forces driving competitive intensity began their ongoing acceleration. Toyota and Southwest weren't the first to leverage technology, but they were so far ahead of their competitors in business innovation and operations that when they made IT integral to their core competencies, it became yet another source of leverage. Southwest, for instance, was not one of the first airlines to sell and market its company through the Internet but has since effectively exploited the opportunity to streamline service and reduce administrative costs. Having built the lead, Southwest sustains it opportunistically and consistently. As long as it can continue to evolve its business model so that it holds up amid changing environmental and competitive forces, Southwest can push its lead and adapt any new resource to its existing platforms, business, process, technology, and value web. Once a leader successfully fuses components and platform—businesses process, technology, and culture—catching up becomes increasingly difficult for competitors.

Urgency is most important in the executive agenda we have outlined in previous chapters.

Componentization

Build Centers of Excellence

Many of the firms we analyzed drove their innovation through small groups that were more than task forces and teams but less than business units. Cemex calls it "The Business Process Center of Excellence," composed of experienced business managers assigned to drive process excellence across the firm, supported by IT staff and specialists in such areas as change management and process analysis.

Our first recommendation is to get moving on componentization via process-focused centers of excellence.

Components are capabilities if and only if they provide value to the company, a center of excellence with a standardized interface. Whether your centers of excellence are composed of activities that will differentiate you in the marketplace or simply drive efficiency through standardization and simplification, you must get started down this road today. However, we needn't tell you that you should not build centers of excellence in areas where there are already capabilities you can source from skilled outside service providers.

All the leading companies we profile started by building their equivalent of centers of excellence: Toyota in design and manufacturing, Amazon in online stores and fulfillment, FedEx in package management and sorting, and Wal-Mart in logistics. Cemex focused on nine specific processes that now make it a leader in the manufacture of cement. For Li & Fung, success depends on its ability to manage quality, schedules, transportation, and vendor relationships. Standardizing the interface was a natural evolution as each company sought to extend the reach of its centers of excellence, whether to value web partners or even only for internal use, but the result was a component. As in GE and eBay, standardization of process became a priority, a goal that is ultimately practical only through standardization of interfaces.

Centers of excellence enable several innovations.

- Functional executives can focus on building their own centers of excellence, which spreads the load, enabling componentization to proceed as a set of parallel activities.

- It enables executives other than the CEO to start the Let Go to Grow process, using their centers to demonstrate the concept and prove the payoff.

- It opens the door for value web discussions.

Shouldn't every company consist exclusively of centers of excellence? That is the idea behind the concept of the virtual firm, but with today's demands on time, cost, and quality, it is impossible for any one company to build all the capabilities it needs.

Turn Centers of Excellence into Components

It takes more than saying that an interface is standardized to turn a center of excellence into a component. When was the last time a company's product manual recommended that you call 1-800-ANSWERS to get your problem solved? Was that really all you needed to know to get your question answered? It is what lies behind the interface—the 800 number—that determines the space we call service. You should develop your own company-specific checklist of what really makes a function— a set of activities—a component. Figure 10.1 provides our own list of characteristics.

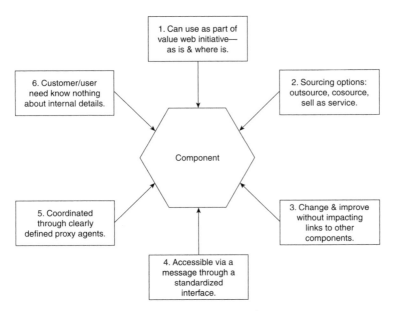

Figure 10.1   The characteristics of components.

Each of these six criteria defines a quality and capability aspect of a component. For instance, if an activity cannot be accessed by a message through a standardized interface (number 5) or is not sufficiently self-contained that it be changed and improved without impacting links to other components, it isn't truly a component. That will be the case for most company activities, in our experience.

Meeting these tests requires both management action and component design, down to the software applications that perform today's business activities and processes. They require training to ensure knowledge and process consistency, as well as design of workflows and responsibilities. It is not a business component unless it is a capability that, above all, is defined *in its use and reuse* through standardized interfaces. Very few of today's business-process design efforts pass the tests; however, tomorrow's component designs must do so if they are to enable platform growth. The central directives of enterprise management then provide the leadership framework and momentum for local innovation and execution. It is far easier for centers of excellence to drive componentization in a firm such as GE or Wal-Mart than in companies that don't quite fit all their services, operations, planning, and logistics pieces together.

You can quickly assess how many of your own company's activities and *business applications* pass the tests listed in Figure 10.1 by considering the following six statements.

- **We can directly use this component as part of a value web initiative**—It can be applied anywhere, not only as it is and where it is. Reuse is a requirement, not an option, of componentization. If a process, function, activity, or business application cannot be reused, it is not a component.

- **We can re-source it fairly directly**—We can outsource or co-source it or make it part of our services. The value of a component comes from how it can be sourced, marketed, or made part of a relationship. Outsourcing a call center is a form of value sourcing *if* the transfer can be made without heavy investment and process change by either the company or its service provider; the test of its being a component is if it can be brought back in-house, should the company so decide—as many componentized firms routinely do and others wish that they could.

- **We can make continued changes and improvements within the component without affecting links to other components or value web players**—In the IT field, which is moving rapidly to support business componentization through component-based software and service-oriented architectures, this is known as encapsulation. The component is self-contained and accessed via a standardized interface. As long as the interface remains standardized, the code can be improved and extended. The same must be true for all aspects of a business component; it can be improved in terms of productivity, its growth productivity increased through process design, and its reuse extended through interface links to other components inside and outside the firm. If these changes affect other components or require that they be altered in order to adapt to the new capability, this is not a component.

- **Others can access it via a standardized message interface**—The "message" generally is based on a formal contract. For example, a purchase order is both a message and a contract. In paper form, it is not a standardized interface; variations in document formats and terminology have for decades been an obstacle to supply chain management. The message can be sent electronically, however, because the two parties have previously established their B2B contractual relationship.

- **It is coordinated through a clearly defined proxy agent**—A component is, by definition, part of a larger whole: a service, process, relationship, or value web. This means that someone must be in charge of coordinating it, with the authority and accountability to handle exceptions, synchronize links and flows, and manage events. In more and more instances, this proxy-agent process will be a piece of software with decision rules embedded in an IT application. We are seeing the emergence of massively complex and powerful real-time systems in supply chain management, financial trading, and manufacturing integration that are a set of these proxies. You can think of a proxy as a notary public, an agent with clearly defined but bounded authority that certifies a document. The business equivalent is the manager/coordinator with authority to accept the message "invoking" a component and certify the transaction.

- **The customer/user need know nothing about the internal details of the component**—When you phone a travel agent to book a flight or use the Web to do so, do you know exactly how the agent or service steps through accessing airline reservation systems, checking availability and price and processing your credit card authorization? Why would you need to know? Why would you care?

The need-to-know issue is core to effective design and deployment of components. A business component is a capability. Defining a component is thus very much a management decision about its *role* as a capability. That decision then determines the degree of operational detail involved in defining and bounding the component. A business component is marked by a trust boundary: "You don't need to know." If you *do* need to know, the component must be broken down into more detailed elements because the power of componentization is that it enables coordination without adding complexity.

Do you know what operating system your personal computer uses? The answer is, of course; you have to know because decisions about software, upgrades, and peripherals change based on which OS you have. Do you know what operating system your mobile phone uses? Did you even think of the phone as having an operating system? The point here is that you don't need to know your cell phone OS; unlike the world of PCs, the mobile phone is componentized and its interfaces standardized. Componentization can be summed up as "out of sight, never on your mind."

Other Rules for Componentization

- Don't componentize if your only objective is to answer the question: Now what should we outsource? This approach will make short work of not only the process but also the value and, ultimately, your company. Outsourcing is an option for some components, but it is a very small part of the overall enterprise answer.

- Define the components at the appropriate level of business detail. If it is a component that will be sourced, the providers of those components will provide the detail required at a relatively high level, including interfaces, messages, and contractual requirements. If this is a component that you plan to keep, make sure that you take planning and design to the level where it produces maximum value for the organization. In the case of TQM, as exemplified by Toyota, every component had to be handled at an exquisite level of precision. It's like coordinating a ballet; no detail is too small.

Look for short-term payoff: You should be able to see payoffs within six months to a year. But you have to plan for componentization and demand success from your team. If you don't do so, this could be another business process reengineering disappointment or ERP cost overrun.

We began our transformation at IBM by attacking the entire organization at once rather than approaching our reengineering sequentially. Most of the work centered on core processes that dealt with the outside world, including hardware and software development, fulfillment, integrated supply chain, and customer relationship management and services. The rest focused on internal processes, namely, human resources, procurement, finance, real estate, and our information technology infrastructure. IBM set short-term milestones and metrics to drive fast results, and from 1994 to 1998, the total saving from these transformation projects was $9.5 billion. From 1994 through 2003, IBM's transformation realized $17.4 billion in benefits from $6.4 billion in investment. For us, this has and remains a journey, and as we move into the on demand phase of our transformation, our focus has moved beyond simply driving efficiencies to enabling top-line revenue growth.

Two more thoughts:

- Make the process iterative, from governance, to components building, to the enterprise technology platform and back. This is a learning process for everyone in the organization.

- Architect and build your technology platform simultaneous to the componentization of your business.

Technology

Coordinate Your Technology

Coordination is essential to business componentization, and information technology itself provides component pieces, fits component pieces together, and synchronizes their access and use. Although technology planning and implementation should not be the responsibility of business managers, technology is part of their governance role: providing the policies and rules to ensure that technology is handled on an appropriately enterprisewide scale.

Everything in IT is now helping the business-componentization process. The underlying base is a service-oriented architecture platform built to ensure services as needed, when needed, and where needed. Contrast this with the old days of large-scale software and data applications: systems as available, run at fixed times, and accessible only within narrow limits. The entire information technology industry is moving to components—to component technology that supports componentized business. For decades, companies could not componentize processes and services, because they depended on rigid IT processing systems and application-dependent processes, and couldn't agree on the definition of even such elementary items as "customer." Fortunately, all this is changing quickly. It is one of the forces moving componentization from manufactured goods to services and then to processes.

We emphasize two governance points here.

- Most companies are poorly positioned to exploit IT's componentization opportunity, because their managers do not view IT as a component of their businesses or understand the relationship between desired business capabilities and the enterprise technology base. They increasingly focus on the many elements of IT that are generic and nondifferentiating and race to outsource them.

- It takes time, effort, and investment to map and componentize IT, just as it does to componentize the business.

There is a dangerous view in some areas of business today that IT doesn't matter and that it offers no competitive advantage.[1] This view lulls business managers into the delusion that they can get the best of IT capability from outsourcing. They can't.

By contrast, we believe that there is *every* advantage to be gained by coordinating IT as a three-level enterprise resource, as shown in Figure 10.2.

```
┌─────────────────────────────────────────────────┐
│                 Superstructure                  │
│                                                 │
│             Unique competitive advantage:       │
│   ✓ Priority targets: customer relationships,   │
│     supply chain, financial, organizational,    │
│     operational                                 │
│   ✓ Branding                                    │
│   ✓ Innovation paths                            │
│   ✓ Bundling of distinctive capabilities via    │
│     components and platform                      │
│   ✓ Value web differentiators                   │
├─────────────────────────────────────────────────┤
│                 Infrastructure                  │
│                                                 │
│           Standard business configuration:      │
│   ✓ Cluster of components                       │
│   ✓ Networks of partners and providers          │
├─────────────────────────────────────────────────┤
│                  Substructure                   │
│                                                 │
│           Highly standardized foundation:       │
│   ✓ Heat, power, & lights                       │
│   ✓ Web for communications (like electricity)   │
│   ✓ Common interfaces                           │
│   ✓ Largely variable-cost bases                 │
└─────────────────────────────────────────────────┘
```

Figure 10.2   The new enterprise IT platform.
(Adapted from "The Components of Value Networks" from *Cutter IT Journal*, Vol. 16, No. 8, p. 29, August 2003. Reprinted by permission.)

The increasingly componentized *substructures* of IT are the parts that are ubiquitous, taken for granted, and available on a utility basis. It is the equivalent of electricity in the home: absolutely standardized components and interfaces. The standard PC, telecommunications links, and common spreadsheet export formats are examples of IT substructures. Platform components, such as low-end and midrange servers and disk storage, exemplify the commoditization of previously premium products, now interchangeable parts.

IT *infrastructures* are technical capabilities that add integration: reach and range.[2] *Reach* is the extent to which other parties—internal users, suppliers, customers, and other value web partners—can access your systems. *Range* is the extent to which componentized applications and other information resources can be automatically and directly accessed and leveraged. The infrastructure also dictates the reliability, scalability, and extensibility of the componentized resources. The major shift in IT over the past few years has been the shift from a company-specific, non-componentized infrastructure to components based on open standards and built with standardized interfaces.

Business *superstructures* are where IT really matters. Firms that grow their value webs build process and service capabilities upon their IT infrastructures. The infrastructure does not create the capability—an assumption that many companies make. These companies spend millions of dollars on packages for customer relationship management, supply chain management, and knowledge management, but it's their pervasive use in the organization that creates a capability. The leaders focus on core business processes, the choice and design of their components, their coordination capabilities, and the building of their culture. Then they use IT to build something that matters.

Your immediate priority is to get rid of generic IT components that offer no differentiation. Seek out scarce global technology talent through specialization of services, because IT talent remains very scarce in many areas of noncommodity development and innovation. A company with a first-rate global platform should access talent where it can. It should consolidate and standardize its components that do not add competitive differentiation and seek competitive superiority in the remaining areas. Superiority comes from fusing business and technology to bundle components, such as supply chain management and customer relationship management.

Coordinating Enterprise Technology

Amazon.com illustrates the fusion of substructure, infrastructure, and superstructure IT capabilities with its powerful growth engine. The "IT doesn't matter" proponents state that Amazon is using universally available, open standards, so that any company can do the same and that every smart retailer is moving toward the same process and technology infrastructures. We agree. But we know the harsh reality: You won't achieve your business goals without componentization. Even the most anti-IT advocate cannot explain Amazon's uniqueness without admitting that what an organization does with IT really does make a difference.

At the *substructure* layer, Amazon's online business is composed of all the same tools that any other online business can utilize. Yet many firms, weary of IT hype, spent millions of dollars on ERP systems and

Y2K updates and then ended up writing off failed projects. They see little apparent payoff from their technology investments and are choosing not to exploit the substructure componentization opportunity. Instead, they freeze IT investment and outsource the entire technology operation.

Amazon's business is based on the Internet or, rather, on the open standards and interfaces that are built around existing Internet technology; loosely termed Web Services, they are components. The Internet is how customers find Amazon, choose the products they want to buy, and transact a sale. The Internet also links Amazon with thousands of partners, and Amazon runs its servers on Linux, the open source operating system. Until very recently, Amazon relied exclusively on external search engine services—components—such as Google and Yahoo!, to drive its traffic. As we discussed earlier, Amazon is also using the XML and SOAP Web Services standards to connect with 30,000 independent developers who are creating new services for both Amazon and the online community.

All these substructure services are absolutely essential to Amazon but in no way differentiate it from any other online business. They are open, easy to access, and either come free or can be purchased largely on a pay-as-you-go model.

At the *infrastructure* level, Amazon has a componentized business model. Its technology and process base have clean, standardized interfaces that enable the search components to link to the selling components, which interface to a number of different fulfillment components, which link to FedEx or UPS for shipping. Other components handle financial transactions, forecasting and planning, and accounting. Amazon is a very componentized business. If it weren't, Amazon could not have formed its partner relationship with Borders, whereby a customer can start at either Amazon.com or Borders.com to reach the Amazon web site. Customers who come in through Borders.com, however, can opt to pick up their book purchases at a local Borders retail store.

This level of integration requires that Amazon be enabled to not only check the inventory in its own distribution centers but also Borders inventory at each local store. It also requires options for both the fulfillment and the revenue-collection processes—in one case, collecting a commission; in the other, handling payment through its normal procurement and billing system. Without a component-based structure, there is no way that Amazon could do this with Borders or its thousands of other partners. Most companies go through a lot of pain to form a much more limited number of relationships. It's the value of componentization.

The component-based infrastructure is essential but not sufficient. It takes Amazon's platform capabilities at the superstructure layer to really make this work smoothly. Security, reliability, scalability—handling volume growth—and speed are as much substructure requirements as is electricity. We expect the power to be on and stay on, and Amazon is now a power company in this regard.

> *Online means always on. Services means always reliable. On demand means always available.*

In addition, the infrastructure layer defines Amazon's many relationship management capabilities: databases that hold the customer information; middleware and application programming interfaces that enable Amazon to transact business with customers lacking the latest standards, routers, and servers that are scalable and guarantee up-time; application software to do accounting and link to the financial institutions that clear credit card transactions; and additional tools that allow Amazon to manage the hundreds of components required to run a business.

Notwithstanding the previous, it is the *superstructure* layer that sets Amazon apart. This includes its IT *services* that enabled it to create the Borders partnership almost overnight, offer an apparel store with 400 retailers within a unified storefront, sell and fulfill toys for Toys "R" Us while Toys "R" Us selects, buys, and manages the inventory, and launch a new jewelry store that offers goods at an extraordinarily low 15 percent markup. Amazon's platform provides the *tools* that enable its partners to create and manage their own content while adhering to

Amazon's "single-store" structure, quality, and response time. It includes fulfillment management software to maximize picking, sorting, and packing efficiency and to decide what items come from what warehouse and if and where consolidation should occur. Without these capabilities, Amazon could not afford its free-shipping offer. This was a core factor in the firm's maintaining its growth targets when Internet commerce went through a cyclic slowdown. The superstructure helps Amazon create new customer services such as "search inside the book," a capability that included unveiling a new search engine.

This is only a small fraction of Amazon's enterprise technology base, a base that started with a fairly standard Internet substructure. On top of that, Amazon added a very robust process and service infrastructure. Neither of these set it apart, but they enabled the superstructure that makes Amazon a formidable competitor, a company that has built the structure needed to let it let go and grow. It is the base for rapid and continuous development to keep Amazon competitive.

Horizontal Versus Vertical Integration

The flexibility allowed by horizontal integration, technology, and leadership are strongly linked. Componentizing the business and the associated technology base produces speed, flexibility, adaptability, and cost optionality, if you follow the component guidelines described in Figure 10.1. The value web roles that your company can play will be limited, however, without the right leadership and governance rules.

Horizontal integration expands value web opportunities and enables you to exploit components. Speed, flexibility, and adaptability facilitate the strengthening of a control web; they are efficiency productivity in action. In this role, you are concerned mainly with your internal agility, and your technology platform must reflect that focus. To the extent that you coordinate or collaborate outside, you can dictate the terms of the standards and interfaces. The role of coordinator opens up new value web spaces but also puts new demands on your technology platform because your company can no longer dictate the terms of coordination, which forces its platform to be based on industry coordination standards.

As you move to the service role, your collaboration priorities move from internal to external. Because you are working with a limited number of partners, however, your external collaboration capabilities are based on the needs of your clients, which means that your firm's platform must adapt to and adopt their choice of standards.

The collaboration role dictates that you must be able to coordinate with anyone, and you must be able to collaborate with anyone, anytime, a new dimension of platform requirements.

The last move is to becoming the enabler of innovation. Up to this point, your company's growth opportunity is dependent primarily on your internal innovation. As a collaborator, however, if you want to enable others to innovate with you, you must open up your own components and platform so that others can innovate on your behalf. Open standards are inevitable for the growth firm.

Speed in a Control value web becomes an even bigger asset in the more complex world of an enabling web; it is the difference between time to complete an operation and time to introduce an innovation to the market. The flexibility generated by horizontal integration moves a company from Control to Enable, not in a single leap but more sustainably as business evolution.

Iterating: Governance and Componentization

With new technologies and standards; such as the Internet, Web Services, and service-oriented architecture, it is easy to underestimate the amount of work and investment required to build and enhance your technology platform. After all, aren't we talking about a set of components, PCs, servers, databases, networks, and now the Internet and Web Services? Yes, but anyone who has built a house knows the time and effort it takes to turn 2×4s, electrical boxes, and sheet rock—the components of a construction project—into a home. Those same components can be used to build a $150,000 house, a $3 million house, or two very different $400,000 houses. Governance rules define the needs of the business just as requirements define the needs of the homebuyer. But our example is too simplistic, because the enterprise IT platforms of a large firm are more analogous to a city rather than simply a house. Houses are built out of components, whereas coordinating all the transportation links, utilities, zoning ordinances, policing, emergency services, and other aspects of a well-managed city demand complex planning, design, and implementation. The same is very much the case for the IT business "city" of modern business.

Because your business is always changing, your platform must continuously evolve. In 2000, Amazon.com was displaying merchandise in different virtual stores, depending on whether the merchandise was sold directly or offered by one of its many partners. At that point, the Amazon executive team decided that it could not meet its growth and mission objectives if it continued down the path of different stores. As a result, the team decided that Amazon would have a single, unified store that would display goods sold by everyone that Amazon did business with. That decision changed not only the storefront components but also the coordination between the components, including order management, payments, and fulfillment. Had Amazon not built a componentized, horizontally integrated platform from the very beginning, they would not have been able to implement this massive strategic and architectural change. The impact of that decision on the technology platforms of most companies would have stopped that implementation dead in its tracks.

Another example is FedEx. FedEx started as an express package-delivery business and invested heavily in the technology needed to support that business. As it expanded into freight, ground, and now the Kinko's copy and information-exchange business, it has had to make many conscious platform-investment choices about what to standardize and centralize. Had it not been able to evolve its technology platform, FedEx would have been much more limited in its business options.

CEO Fred Smith explains how FedEx decides what processes and systems it standardizes, what it allows to vary across geographies and operating units, and how it enforces the decisions that call for standardization. Here is how Fred explained the Fed Ex solution:

We have a unique strategy: Operate independently, compete collectively, and manage collaboratively.[3] This means each of our core operating companies—FedEx Express, FedEx Ground, FedEx Freight, and FedEx Kinko's—gears its systems and processes to the particular segment it serves. When it comes to our markets, one size does not fit all. So each company tailors its service and operations to its specific customer needs. At the same time, our operating companies compete collectively under the trusted FedEx name. That means certain standards are met, no matter which service a customer is using. For example, all our team members— couriers, contractors, service reps on the telephone—are asked to keep the Purple Promise to our customers; that is, to give them the best experience possible any time they use FedEx.

Frequent communications, rewards, and recognition of excellent behavior, along with building accountability into management objectives, let FedEx achieve consistent customer experiences across companies, services, and countries.

This dynamic picture of FedEx highlights that standardization is not bureaucracy but the coordination of the enterprise to facilitate innovation at any level and in any place. The coordinated technology platform that has always been part of FedEx's competitive differentiation supports and leverages this business dynamic and lets FedEx innovate and grow.

The complexity of technology and the absolute requirement that it be tailored to meet the needs of the business mean that governance and componentization must always move in synchronization. Sometimes, governance will drive new componentization initiatives, and sometimes, componentization initiatives will shape platform decisions. The lack of platform capability, however, must never block componentization and cross-linking of components, as it has so often in the past. If this governance and componentization are not carefully synchronized, organizational, technical, and cultural rigidities will impede the move from the control value chain model to more open and extensive value webs. Figure 10.3 illustrates the point as a reminder that this coordination is driven by leadership and built on enterprise productivity targets.

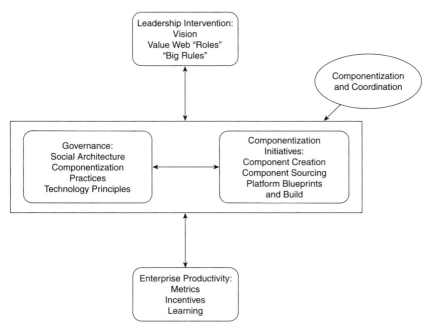

Figure 10.3   Synchronizing the business components.

First-Mover Advantage

Many of the technology leadership books available today discuss first-mover advantage or the lack thereof. Some observers claim that there is no first-mover advantage and that it is far better to be a fast follower, letting the leaders take the arrows and learn from their mistakes. When a leader claims a space and continuously works to improve it, the competitors have a difficult time even competing, let alone catching up. From 1987, Wal-Mart was 44 percent more productive, as measured by revenue per employee, than the rest of the industry. By 1995, it was 48 percent more productive. By 1999, the rest of the industry was emulating Wal-Mart's logistics processes and had implemented many of the same technologies, yet Wal-Mart was still 41percent more productive.

Platforms are difficult to build, and those firms that choose to differentiate through components, by building industry-leading platforms and then continuing to enhance them, are difficult to unseat. If you want to have flexibility in your business space, move early or be willing to move to where the leaders aren't already established.

A Template Approach to Componentization

Componentization needs maps. A map is not a reality but a way of categorizing, labeling, and orienting so that teams can navigate their way ahead. Sometimes, such maps are termed "methodology," "framework," or "models," and there are books, companies, and gurus offering them to your firm every day. The exact term is less important than the purpose: to provide a shared and structured mapping process. Rather than try to review the maps we have seen companies use, however, we'll share one that has proved to be useful in a number of business componentization contexts.

Figure 10.4 shows a template approach to mapping business components that has helped several companies orient themselves, plan their journey, and get moving. It shows a Component Business Model (CBM) for the consumer products business as generated by IBM Business Consulting Services. There typically appear to be 50–60 business components per industry—hence, the initial complexity of the figure. This is not an absolute value, because each of the components, such as Consumer Service or Plant Inventory Management, can often be decomposed into more atomistic components or combined with others to form bundled services. The map we offer is thus a template, a starting point for an in-depth adaptive review of an individual firm's componentization opportunities and options.

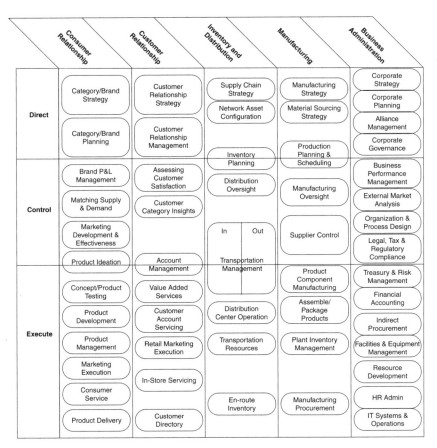

	Consumer Relationship	Customer Relationship	Inventory and Distribution	Manufacturing	Business Administration
Direct	Category/Brand Strategy	Customer Relationship Strategy	Supply Chain Strategy	Manufacturing Strategy	Corporate Strategy
			Network Asset Configuration	Material Sourcing Strategy	Corporate Planning
					Alliance Management
	Category/Brand Planning	Customer Relationship Management		Production Planning & Scheduling	Corporate Governance
			Inventory Planning		
Control	Brand P&L Management	Assessing Customer Satisfaction	Distribution Oversight		Business Performance Management
				Manufacturing Oversight	External Market Analysis
	Matching Supply & Demand	Customer Category Insights			
					Organization & Process Design
	Marketing Development & Effectiveness		In Out	Supplier Control	Legal, Tax & Regulatory Compliance
	Product Ideation	Account Management	Transportation Management	Product Component Manufacturing	Treasury & Risk Management
Execute	Concept/Product Testing	Value Added Services			Financial Accounting
			Distribution Center Operation	Assemble/ Package Products	
	Product Development	Customer Account Servicing			Indirect Procurement
	Product Management	Retail Marketing Execution	Transportation Resources	Plant Inventory Management	Facilities & Equipment Management
	Marketing Execution				Resource Development
	Consumer Service	In-Store Servicing			
			En-route Inventory	Manufacturing Procurement	HR Admin
	Product Delivery	Customer Directory			IT Systems & Operations

Figure 10.4   A component business model. (Source: IBM Business Consulting Services.)

Jeff Neville, one of the originators of this CBM mapping technique at IBM, describes his team's experiences applying it at one of the world's largest consumer products companies: "The firm's leadership was becoming increasingly concerned that 'doing more of the same wasn't cutting it' and that they needed to change the game."[4] Jeff's team offered the model as a point of view, a catalyst for new thinking. Ten senior executives attended workshops that explored the opportunities created by componentized thinking. After the workshop, almost all of the executives saw that componentization was inevitable for the consumer goods business and essential for their firm.

As the executives looked at their capabilities across the organization, many focused on the benefit of outsourcing the nondifferentiating parts of the company. Jeff's team used the CBM approach and insights to expand their thinking, to look beyond simply cost reduction to show how componentization can be used to create a growth platform for the entire company and allow it to become the coordinator of its own value web.

What if you want to play a service role in more than one business partner's value webs? Your partners' industry maps should then be examined in addition to your own. Your partners' maps provide you with insight into components that will allow you to differentiate your value web relationships with them.

The maps provide the big picture, enabling you to work through the component value matrix depicted in Figure 10.5.

- **Differentiating versus nondifferentiating**—Is this business component one that helps your company stand out from the pack? Or is it one that is a necessary part of operations that simply has to be done well to keep up with the competition?

- **Specific versus generic**—Is this a capability that requires company-specific skills and processes or one that every company in our competitive ecosystem handles in the same way?

Each of these differentiated components requires a differentiated response, as shown in Figure 10.5.

Component/Value Matrix		
	Nondifferentiating	Differentiating
Specific to the Company	Consolidate & Drive Centers of Excellence (Account Management)	Achieve Competitive Superiority (Category/Brand Strategy)
Generic to the Industry	Manage as Utility (IT Operational)	Leverage Specialists (Advertisement Creation)

Figure 10.5   Maximizing the value of component capabilities.
(Source: IBM Business Consulting Services.)

The bottom-left quadrant in Figure 10.5 is componentization-as-commoditization: generic, standardized, with few variations, non-differentiating, literally a commodity with no competitive value. It is an obvious target for utility sourcing: outsourcing to a firm that offers a service value web. One of the most basic elements of competitive positioning is to exploit these on demand resources with basic information technology operations as a priority target.

Where a component is generic but provides some competitive differentiation for the company (the bottom-right quadrant), it needs to seek out specialists. This might be the use of agencies to place TV and newspaper ads, for example. Many of the examples of industry outsourcing are much more the search for specialized global talent than the search for competitive differentiation. Eli Lilly's InnovCenter is an example here. Rather than outsourcing its R&D, Lilly is in-sourcing skills that it does not have in-house. InnovCenter is a brilliant solution that reflects how research-problem solutions come from unlikely sources, such as a lawyer in North Carolina or a professor in a far-flung region of the old Soviet republics. A company coordination web whose platform can link to those of specialists offers a powerful growth capability.

The top row of Figure 10.5 addresses nongeneric components, ones that are specific to the firm. The top-left quadrant is a major opportunity for innovation through more efficient business processes. Here the components offer no competitive differentiation, but they are company specific. The main opportunities for reuse, re-sourcing, and bundling are internal to the firm. Consumer goods account management and manufacturing procurement for all plants are examples of these components. HR policies and processes that relate to national, regional, or local factors or internal budgeting and control systems are more common examples. The sourcing strategy tends toward centralization, simplification, and standardization of processes; we cite GE and eBay as examples. Many companies are now building centers of excellence to componentize processes and move them out across the organization as best practice.

The fourth quadrant in the diagram is the one that is most clearly related to competitive advantage: firm-specific capabilities that differentiate the firm in its business ecosystem. The goal must be to build competitive superiority. Think brand management in consumer goods. In both the auto industry and consumer electronics, design is increasingly the path to industry leadership.

If we think of a value web as a portfolio of capabilities, the four quadrants are a source of opportunities. The basic rules for a coordinator web are as follows.

- Seek out a utilitylike service for handling generic components that offer no competitive differentiation. Your company gains the edge in speed, flexibility, adaptation, and cost optionality at the component level, while removing an organizational and economic burden.

- Bring specialists into your value web for generic business components that provide differentiation. Here, the edge comes from coordination and collaboration through horizontal integration. This also opens up the type of relationship opportunity that Magna, TAL, Li & Fung, and IBM offer.

- Where a component is specific to your firm but provides no competitive differentiation, use a Center of Excellence approach, and make it a reusable asset.

- For the firm-specific differentiating components, seek competitive superiority in every way you can—hiring, process design, patents, training, and leadership—while strengthening the portfolio capabilities that support and enhance them. BMW retains its design differentiation while using Magna as its manufacturing specialist. P&G complements its in-house brand management and marketing firm–specific capabilities with access to specialists in research and utility outsourcing of HR administration and manufacturing.

The basic rules vary by pivot point or the value web role you see your company playing as you build your growth platform. For instance, if your pivot point is service, you will not only be looking for componentized capabilities in your own business, but also will be focusing on the bottom row; look to key partners for opportunities to build new capabilities that foster your own growth.

Summary

We have presented a sequence of management principles that can help any company turn the commodity threat into a growth opportunity. The principles are broad and must be tailored to your specific company context. Each of our principles poses many individual challenges: cultural change, planning, design, and implementation. The mainstream of business is increasingly moving to competition through standardized interfaces, and commoditization is the inevitable result, creating a double bind; the company that componentizes is in effect entering a marathon such that every few miles, an extra weight is placed on its back. On the other hand, we passionately believe that the ones that do not componentize are left out of the race entirely.

Componentization is the key to business context change in the coming years and to companies' response to that context. Your firm must componentize, but it must also coordinate its componentization. The key is to take a platform view and ensure that leadership and governance both help enable the platform.

If innovation were easy, every company would be an innovator. It isn't easy. But in today's environment, the question is not whether to innovate but how.

The initial management challenge is to get started.

11

GAINING THE COLLABORATION EDGE: BUILDING THE CREATIVE COMPANY FOR THE CREATIVE ECONOMY

We began this book by showing the commoditization cycle and the two basic competitive responses: cost-cutting retrenchment or letting go to grow. In many competitive ecosystems, we are only beginning to see the signs of the commoditization that has transformed consumer electronics, manufacturing, telecommunications, retailing, and financial services. We anticipate an accelerating pace of change in pharmaceuticals, media, education, healthcare, construction, and travel. The deconstruction and reconstruction of these business systems is a global phenomenon.

This business evolution could not be happening without a global talent base accessible through high-speed telecommunications. The educational systems of many other countries have caught up with North America and Europe, and their elites are graduates of our U.S.-based academic programs. Over half of all advanced technical degrees awarded by U.S. universities go to foreign students. In many areas of engineering and IT, foreign high schools and colleges are also producing skilled specialists who are at the other end of a customer-support hotline or help desk.

Much of what is called outsourcing is actually more akin to *in*sourcing talent. In the commodity areas of customer service and technical support, for example, the insourcing/outsourcing activity is based on accessing good skills at minimal cost. When you're targeting growth and innovation, your strategy is based on accessing the *best* skills, regardless of where they are. This is what Richard Florida aptly calls the Creative Economy.[1]

We'll consider the intersection and interaction of all the commoditization and componentization forces that result from access to a global talent base. We will outline our ideas not for specific business strategies but for a metastrategy—a strategy for defining strategies—that positions you to leverage the global talent base and secure a place in the new business ecosystem.

The Creative Economy

In 1999, the Creative Class made up 30 percent of the U.S. workforce, and the percentage was growing in both the United States and globally. These workers identify with their profession and community, not the company that employs them. They move to cities and regions that encourage their sense of innovation; provide access to communities that help support, reinforce, and extend their creative work; and reward their talent. They change jobs every 3.5 years. They avoid becoming part of the commodity labor pool and look at the increasing options offered by companies that source jobs globally, even though most of them still want "real" jobs because freelancing is difficult.[2]

This mobility and flexibility have immense political and social implications, social and economic impact, and a direct influence on policy choices. Some observers see outsourcing as a crisis that is destroying the very fabric of labor markets and dissolving the professional workforce, whereas others demonstrate how component sourcing generates domestic jobs and that every dollar spent on sourcing returns approximately $1.20 to the national economy.[3]

There are also heated and passionate arguments about the exact number of domestic workers affected by these changes.

The underlying issues in this debate center on creativity, innovation, and the roles that value webs can play in sourcing innovation. There can be no question that componentization leads to the relocation of work to companies, geographic regions, and economies best able to attain the optimal mix of cost, quality, and talent. A firm that is involved only in coordinating value webs but not taking part in innovation and creativity value webs may well find itself in commodity hell anyway.

The Creative Economy also takes advantage of the trend toward commoditization as companies look for new ways to innovate. Consider Nokia and Apple as examples. Both have used design as a creative edge, a strategic differentiator in highly componentized market segments. By contrast, Timken, TAL, and FedEx cannot grow their businesses except through commoditization and componentization, so their creative edge comes from process invention. In the consumer electronics field, research, design, commoditization, and componentization combine to drop prices, enhance quality, and push innovation. The customer benefits from value webs built around the symbiotic relationship among coordinator firms, collaborators, service players, and enablers.

The metastrategy of the winning firms is to ensure that they have restructured their businesses to leverage the emerging Creative Economy, with its talent pools, laboratories, and alliances. These will be global because the creative talent is global. In many instances, these firms will keep jobs in the United States or Europe and either hire talent abroad by setting up new operations or extend their value web relationships to create new overseas collaborations. Leading universities continue to attract technical talent from all over the globe, for example, and some stay in the university community, working at either the college or a nearby business. Others opt to return home when their studies are complete, filling standard jobs; still others take their list of contacts with them and become entrepreneurs, drawing on these networks of connections to create new businesses.

Jobs will not simply be moved from one region to another, but the overall composition of the global workforce will continue to evolve. China lost a higher percentage of manufacturing jobs than did the

United States between 1996 and 2002: U.S. manufacturing jobs declined 11.3 percent;[4] China's decreased 15.3 percent.[5] This may come as a surprise to readers who believe that "Made in China" and "Sold in the U.S." are the basis of today's inflation-busting retail climate. In this same period, global industrial output increased by 30 percent, with most of this increase reflecting the commoditization cycle and componentization.

There is really nothing new in this combination of output growth and job loss. For "manufacturing," substitute "agriculture," and the parallel becomes obvious. As recently as 1900, 38 percent of the U.S. labor force worked in agriculture, and most countries relied on their domestic farmers for food production. Now, farming in the United States employs less than 1 percent of the domestic labor pool.[6]

The same factors that caused this change in farming have also been driving the globalization of manufacturing for decades. In this new century, the comparable globalization of service jobs has already begun, especially in the back office; todays there's a lot of administration and document processing work in Slovenia, Mexico, Jamaica, and Toronto, for example. This transformation of service work cannot be stopped, because it is driven by historical forces, not situational ones, as was the transformation in both farming and manufacturing.

Which brings us back to the Creative Economy. Many countries will grow because of their role as component providers, with India, the Philippines, China, and Indonesia all serving as leading examples. India and China also innovate through their growing pool of well-educated managers, engineers, and information technology specialists. One Indian firm, for example, employs 6,500 people who focus on R&D projects for other companies, including nine of the top ten telecommunications equipment manufacturers. Bangalore is a center of the global Creative Economy, not a spoke in the Commodity Economy.

The Creative Economy doesn't include only designers, writers, and engineers but also people in healthcare, law, teaching, manufacturing, and many other areas—creative professionals. This class is creative in its reliance on initiative, speed, flexibility, adaptability, collaboration, coordination, and invention.

There are many recent studies that examine the creative *business* econ-omy. One, carried out in 2001, concluded, "most fast-growing entrepre-neurial companies are not in high-tech industries" but "rather widely distributed across all industries."[7] A 2004 article argues in favor of the everyday innovation that we have discussed in earlier chapters: "rather than focus on chasing wonderful new products, big companies should focus on making lots of small improvements."[8] From established old-economy companies to new-economy Internet players, creativity in process design, value web relationships, and customer service must be everyday priorities.

Growth platforms make both the search for and utilization of global creative talent location-independent. Consider the evolution of InnovCenter, Eli Lilly's creative value web invention that is now a glob-al market for R&D talent. One article, describing a vexing chemical-synthesis problem that was solved in three days by a Kazakhstani scientist, concludes with " have no doubt that scientific smarts are truly global…these days it matters less where you live than whether you have the talent and knowledge people want."[9]

The central issue for business growth is innovation, and for continuous innovation, companies must link to global talent via value webs. As the consumer electronics, mobile phone, and personal computer markets have gone through the commoditization cycle, the edge has visibly moved to the areas of design and process creation, the heart of the cre-ative platform. As Timken, Wal-Mart, and Southwest show, no matter how commoditized a firm's business ecosystem becomes, it can still grow profitably through process creativity.

> *The Creative Class includes everyone in the com-pany, and the potential talent base includes everyone whom the value web can reach.*

Instead of thinking of globalization in terms of win-lose outsourcing, we need to begin viewing it as a long-term shift in the talent portfolio of the labor force. Table 11.1 shows the change in talent in the United States[10] since 1950, exactly illustrating our point.

Table 11.1 U.S. Class Structure

United States Class Stucture		
	1950	1999
Creative Class	16.6%	30.0%
Service Class	30.5%	43.4%
Working Class	41.1%	26.1%
Agriculture	11.8%	<0.5%

The same trends apply worldwide. As China loses manufacturing jobs, it adds others in more creative areas of business. InnovCenter worked with Moscow State University and the Chinese Academy of Sciences to build its talent pool of more than 50,000 scientists in 150 countries. At the start of 2004, the largest single group of scientists in the program was in the United States but in June 2004, China took the lead.

Any local, regional, national, or global shift in the composition of the labor force is inevitably disruptive. The pace, scale, and reach of the commoditization cycle are causing immense stress for workers in many companies. The same happened with the transition from the agricultural to the industrial economy, from the industrial to the service economy, and now from the services economy to the information age. Education has emerged as the real wealth of nations, and for individuals, education is now the equivalent of a financial investment portfolio that builds their lifetime capital and provides their income yield.

> *An essential skill for all 21st-century employees is the ability to deal with people.*

Dealing with people is the foundation of the Creative Economy. InnovCenter finds people and provides client companies with the tools needed to work with firms around the globe. The successes and failures of offshoring call centers and technology help desks rest on the quality of the people and the customer-agent dialog coordinated by the platform. But if you want innovation, coordination is not enough! Process innovation in supply chains and customer services rests on collaboration, as do other effective value web relationships in the Creative Economy.

We began this book with a promise that you would get specific details of what you need to change *today* to remain a competitive firm in the new, global economy, so here are our key points restated.

- *Componentize* your business—Components establish clarity of function and boundaries of operation that ensure appropriate specialization both inside your firm and across your value webs, and the best people pick the best partners. Componentization eliminates your process obstacles, communication ambiguities, data conflicts, and administrative overhead—everything that blocks everyday cooperation and prevents innovative results. It ensures a high standard of performance while also isolating the areas of poor performance, exactly what you and your collaborators need to build a trusted relationship.

- *Integrate* your components end-to-end—The combination of components and platform creates a set of resources that make it worthwhile for partners to identify collaborative innovation opportunities. Your platform provides coordination, the starting point for collaboration. Smoothness in componentization and ease of integration become important assets to collaborators because you can quickly focus on delivering results.

- *Lead* your people to a growth culture—The combination of productivity and collaboration that sparks new innovation will drive sustained revenue growth for your company.

- *Differentiate,* then *integrate*—Collaborators have the best of all worlds with a rich set of components to use, reuse, and resource, along with a platform that makes it simple to deploy them without diverting time, attention, and skills. These firms have also created a cultural bias toward letting go and focusing on value web opportunities—the ability to build very complex process and value web designs via standardized interfaces.[11]

- *Globalize* your workforce—The platform must include both the tools of collaboration and coordination, and diverse talent must be assembled globally and then brought together online to drive innovative results. Highly competitive companies are becoming more skilled at workforce globalization. If you are not exploring the possibilities, you should be.

Is this easy? Of course not. Is it practical? Very much so. Is it worth trying? It's absolutely vital.

The success of your company depends upon it.

The commoditization cycle is influencing every industry, in every country. Will you struggle for control in an increasingly constricting marketplace, or will you Let Go To Grow?

ENDNOTES

Chapter 1

1. *Fortune Magazine*, Fortune 500 Database, 1955–2004. Available online at http://www.fortune.com/fortune/500archive.

2. *Forbes Magazine*, Business Lists. Online at http://www.forbes.com/lists/.

3. Coyle, Diane. "Working Paper," Institute of Political and Economic Governance, University of Manchester, December 2003. Online at http://www.ipeg.org.uk/.

4. "New NAM Poll Shows That Despite Tech Advances, Most Manufacturers Still Not Using E-Commerce," Rob Schwarzwalder and Jo-Anne Prokopowicz, included in a press release by National Association of Manufacturers, February 22, 2000.

5. Amazon Corporation, *Annual Report*, 2002.

6. Stundza, Tom. "Steel Pricing Stinks!" *Purchasing Magazine*, 1 May, 2003.

7. Lieber, Ron. *P&G's Not So Secret Agent*, Fast Company, July 2001.

Chapter 2

1. Herrick, Thaddeus, "Plastic Bag Fight Pits U.S. Makers v. U.S. Importers," *Wall Street Journal*, October 10, 2003.

2. A Guide to Collaboration, Demand Solutions, online at www.demandsolutions.com.

3. Buzek, Greg, "The Value of Information," for Retail.com, October 23, 2000.

4. "E-Biz Strikes Again!" *BusinessWeek*, May 10, 2004.

5. Bylinsky, Gene, "Heroes of Manufacturing," *Fortune Magazine*, March 3, 2003.

Chapter 3

1. The discussion of the mortgage industry in this section draws on work by Professor Lynne Markus, summarized in a conference presentation, "The Ambient Industry: IT-Enabled Transformation in the U.S. Home Mortgage Market," April 2004.

2. Bryce, Robert, "Freddie, Fannie Agree to XML Standard," *eWeek*, June 18, 2001.

3. You can learn more about Desktop Originator online: https://desktoporiginator.fanniemae.com/.

4. Palmeri, Christopher, "Mortage Slump? Bring It On," *BusinessWeek*, December 15, 2003.

5. Hagel, John, Loosening Up: How Process Networks Unlock the Power of Specialization, McKinsey & Company, September 2002.

6. Hagel, John, "Leveraging Growth," *Harvard Business Review*, 2002.

7. "Supply Chain Management: How Li & Fung Adds Value," business case study online at http://bctim.wustl.edu/caseStudies/solutiacase.pdf.

8. Ibid.

Chapter 4

1. Keen, Peter, *A Recipe for Business Process Management*, February 2003, online at www.peterkeen.com.

2. "GE Chief Defends Outsourcing, Pension Benefits," *San Francisco Chronicle*, April 28, 2004.

3. IBM Corporation, *Annual Report*, 2004.

4. IBM Business Leadership Forum, 2003.

5. Ibid.

6. Ibid.

7. Ibid.

8. Collins, James, and Porras, Jerry, *Built to Last*, Harper-Collins, 1999.

9. Procter & Gamble Corporation, *Annual Report*, 2001.

10. "P&G CEO Quits Amid Woes," *Money Magazine*, June 8, 2000.

11. "A Catalyst and Encourager of Change," *BusinessWeek*, July 7, 2003.

12. Ibid.

13. *Atlanta Business Journal*, January 1998.

14. *BusinessWeek*, op. cit.

15. "Pushing Pills: Marketing Drugs to Doctors Is Turning into a Tricky Business," *The Economist*, February 13, 2003.

16. Online at www.innocentive.com.

17. Swiss Re Corporation, *Annual Report*, 1997.

18. CSC, *Annual Report*, 2001.

19. Ibid.

Chapter 5

1. Cemex Corporation, *Annual Report*, 2004. Available online at www.cemex.com.

2. *Productivity and Costs, First Quarter 2005, Revised*, Bureau of Labor Statistics, www.bls.gov.

3. Cemex Corporation, *Annual Report*, 1999, *Letter to Stockholders*.

4. Cemex Corporation, *Annual Report*, 2003, *Letter to Stockholders*.

5. Zambrano, Lorenzo, *Remarks*, Deutsche Bank Global Construction Conference, Lyon, France, November 5, 2003.

6. "Detroit Pulls Out All the Stops in 2004 with Record 48 New or Redesigned Launches," *Automotive Digest*, February 9, 2004.

7. Brown, Stuart, "Toyota's Global Body Shop," *Fortune*, February 9, 2004.

8. Ibid.

9. Schifrin, Matthew, "B2B's Back—Bigger, Better and More Focused," *Forbes*, October 4, 2004.

10. "Circuit City's Fix-It Time," *BusinessWeek*, January 20, 2005.

11. Pilcher, James, "UPS Poised to Set Record Thanks to Online Shoppers," Associated Press wire story, December 18, 1999.

12. Benjamin, Matthew, "Out of the Box," *U.S. News and World Report*, January 26, 2004.

13. "UPS Worldwide Logistics 'Tunes Up' Fender Guitar's European Supply Chain," UPS Logistics Group News Release, May 27, 1999.

14. Mortgage Bankers Association, research report. Online at www.mbaa.org.

15. Weintraub, Arlene, "How eToys Could Have Made It," *BusinessWeek*, February 9, 2001.

16. "Look Who's Building Bimmers," *BusinessWeek*, December 1, 2003.

17. Ibid.

18. *IBM RFID Solution for the Midmarket*, IBM Corporation web site. Online at www.ibm.com.

19. IBM Business Leadership Forum, 2003.

20. Ibid.

21. Ibid.

Chapter 6

1. "The Power of Synchronization: The Case of TAL Apparel Group," Deloitte Research Case Study, May 2005.

2. TAL Apparel, Hong Kong General Chamber of Commerce Member Profile. Online at www.chamber.org.hk.

3. "Hip H&M," *BusinessWeek*, November 11, 2002.

4. Kahn, Gabriel, "Made to Measure: Invisible Supplier Has Penney's Shirts All Buttoned Up," *Wall Street Journal*, September 11, 2003.

5. Ibid.

6. Ibid.

7. "P&G: New and Improved," *BusinessWeek*, July 7, 2003.

8. Walton, Sam, *Made in America*, Doubleday, 1992.

9. First Data Corporation, *Annual Report*, 2002.

10. Anthony, Scott, and, Christensen, Clayton, "Do You Know What You Do Best," *The Economist*, December 2003.

11. Amazon Corporation, *Annual Report*, 1999.

12. Amazon Corporation, *Annual Report*, 2000.

13. Amazon Corporation, *Annual Report*, 2001.

14. Hof, Robert D., "Reprogramming Amazon," *BusinessWeek*, December 22, 2003.

15. Southwest Airlines, Corporate History. Online at www.southwest.com.

Chapter 7

1. Drucker, Peter, *The Need for Profit Planning*, Three Sigma. http://www.threesigma.com/profit_planning.htm.

2. General, selling, and administration expenses.

3. Table Sources : Dell Corporation, *Annual Report*, 2003, and Hewlett-Packard Corporation, *Annual Report*, 2003.

4. Magretta, Joan, "The Power of Virtual Integration: An Interview with Dell Computer's Michael Dell," *Harvard Business Review*, March–April 1998.

5. Yahoo! Corporation, *Annual Report*, 2003.

6. Joachim, David, *Secrets of the e-Commerce Elite*, B to B, February, 2002.

7. Pelline, Jeff, *Booksellers Slash Bestsellers*, News.com, May 17, 1999.

8. Shim, Richard, *Dell Cuts Prices Across Range of Products*, News.com, August 20, 2003.

9. Haddad, Charles, "FedEx Gaining on the Ground," *BusinessWeek*, December 16, 2002.

10. Baird, Woody, "FedEx Reports 41 Percent Earnings Gain," AP Newswire story, March 17, 2004.

11. Charles Haddad, op. cit.

Chapter 8

1. Tichy, Noel, *The Leadership Engine*, HarperBusiness, August 2002.

2. "Leading Change When Business Is Good," *Harvard Business Review*, December 2004.

3. Welch, Jack, and Byrne, John, *Jack: Straight from the Gut*, Warner Business, 2003.

4. "A Catalyst and Encourager of Change," *Business Week*, July 7, 2003.

5. Ibid.

6. Levinson, Meridith, *Yet Another Interview with Jeff Bezos*, Darwin, October 2002.

7. Amazon Corporation, *Annual Report*, 1999.

8. Kotter, J. P., "What Leaders Really Do," *Harvard Business Review on Leadership*, Harvard Business School Publishing, 1998.

Chapter 9

1. General Electric Corporation, *Annual Report*, 2001.

2. "Made in America," *Forbes*, April 12, 2004.

Chapter 10

1. Carr, Nicholas, "IT Doesn't Matter," *Harvard Business Review*, May 2003.

2. Dortch, Michael, "Toward the Elastic Enterprise," *CIO*, August 6, 2003.

3. *FedEx: Raising the Bar on Customer Satisfaction*, CapGemini, 2003. Online at web.capgemini.com.

4. Neville, Jeff, personal interview, March 2005.

Chapter 11

1. Florida, Richard, *The Rise of the Creative Class*, Perseus Books, 2002.

2. Ibid.

3. Vaknin, Sam, "The Real Threats to the Economy of the USA," *Global Politician*, April 26, 2005.

4. *What Accounts for the Decline in Manufacturing Employment?*, U.S. Congressional Budget Office Issue Summary, February 18, 2004.

5. Hilsenrath, Jon, and Buckman, Rebecca, "Factory Employment Is Falling Worldwide," *Wall Street Journal*, October 20, 2003.

6. *Briefing Room: Farm Labor*, U.S. Department of Agriculture Economic Research Service, online at www.ers.usda.gov.

7. *Mapping America's Entrepreneurial Landscape*, National Commission on Entrepreneurship, 2001.

8. "Don't Laugh at Gilded Butterflies," *The Economist*, April 24, 2004.

9. Kirkpatrick, David, "Big League R&D Gets Its Own eBay," *Fortune Magazine*, May 3, 2004.

10. Florida, Richard, opt. cit.

11. Majchrzak, Ann, Malhotra, Arvind, Stamps, Jeffrey, and Lipnack, Jessica, "Can Absence Make a Team Grow Strong?" *Harvard Business Review*, May 2004.

INDEX

IBM
    articulating vision through shared values,
        131-134
    componentization, rules for, 165
    on demand concepts, 32
    proprietary interfaces, 28
    workforce optimization, 152
IBM Business Consulting Services, 176
IBM jam, 133
Immelt, Jeff, 49, 147
improving productivity, 150-152
industries
    apparel, 91-92
    automakers. *See* automakers
    decomposition of, 84
    mortgage industries, components, 35-37
Iniguez, Gelacio, 72-73
InnoCentive scientific forum (Eli Lilly), 62
innovation, xvi, 49, 51, 86
    enabling customer and partner
        innovation, 106-107
    growth, 144
    leadership, 3
    productivity in innovative worlds,
        149-150
    success of platforms, 30
InnovCenter, 188
insourcing, 184
integrating components, 2, 76, 78-81
integration, 67, 78, 171-172, 189
interfaces, 28, 55
    standardized electronic interfaces,
        moving to, 56-57
    standardized interfaces, 34-35, 56
Internet, GE, 158
inventory management, Dell, 117
IT
    componentization, 28
    enterprise technology, coordinating,
        168-171
    growth leaders, 158
    productivity, 149
    technology, coordinating, 166-168

J-K

JC Penney, 21, 94-95

kanban, Toyota, 155
Kelleher, Herb, 130
Kinko's, 61, 123

L-M

Lafley, Alan, 52-53, 137
leaders, 129-130
    componentization, 14
    growth leaders, 24-25

leadership, 129-130, 157, 189
    Amazon, 138-139
    articulating the vision through shared
        values, 131-134
    executing visions through collaboration,
        134-135
    GE, 136-137
    innovation, 3
    linking vision to execution, 131
    Procter & Gamble, 137
Lee, Harry, 93-94
Let Go to Grow, xvi, 22-24
leveraging components, 122-124
Li & Fung, 91
    componentization, 38-43
    moving to standardized electronic
        interfaces, 56-57
    value webs, 42, 77
licenses, patents, 53
linking vision to execution, 131
Loan Prospector, Freddie Mac, 36

M&A (mergers and acquisitions), 10
Magna, 56
Magna Steyr, 85-86
managing costs, 11
manufacturing, contract manufacturing, 85
manufacturing jobs, 185
mapping components, 54
markets, creating through collaboration,
    103-105
measuring productivity, 142-144
Mercedes, 85
MISMO, 36
monoliths, 47-48, 61
mortgage industry, components, 35-37
moving
    from control to coordination, 99-101
    to standardized electronic interfaces,
        56-57

N-O-P

Neville, Jeff, 177
Nike, value webs, 39
nondifferentiating versus
    differentiating, 178

on demand business, 14, 26, 32, 170
online, 170
opportunities for growth platforms,
    107-108, 110
options
    for growth platforms, 107-108, 110
    value webs, 83-84
outsourcing, 84, 184
    BMW, 56
    P&G, 53
overhead costs, 121

W-X-Y-Z

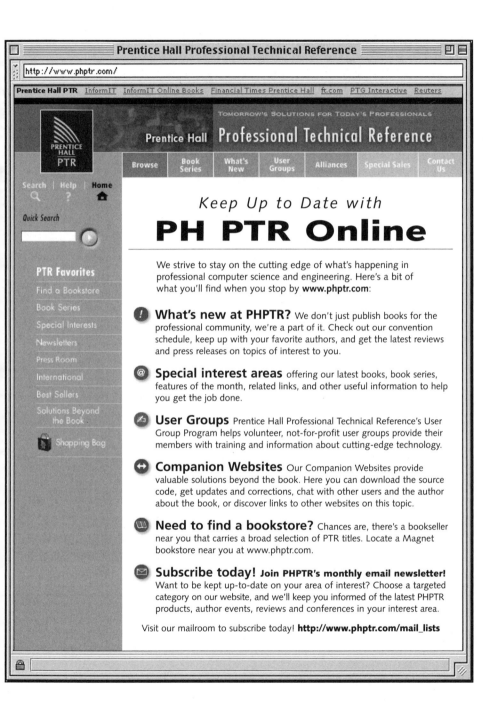

http://www.phptr.com/

Prentice Hall PTR   InformIT   InformIT Online Books   Financial Times Prentice Hall   ft.com   PTG Interactive   Reuters

TOMORROW'S SOLUTIONS FOR TODAY'S PROFESSIONALS

Prentice Hall **Professional Technical Reference**

Browse | Book Series | What's New | User Groups | Alliances | Special Sales | Contact Us

Search | Help | Home

Quick Search

PTR Favorites

Find a Bookstore

Book Series

Special Interests

Newsletters

Press Room

International

Best Sellers

Solutions Beyond the Book

Shopping Bag

Keep Up to Date with
PH PTR Online

We strive to stay on the cutting edge of what's happening in professional computer science and engineering. Here's a bit of what you'll find when you stop by **www.phptr.com**:

What's new at PHPTR? We don't just publish books for the professional community, we're a part of it. Check out our convention schedule, keep up with your favorite authors, and get the latest reviews and press releases on topics of interest to you.

Special interest areas offering our latest books, book series, features of the month, related links, and other useful information to help you get the job done.

User Groups Prentice Hall Professional Technical Reference's User Group Program helps volunteer, not-for-profit user groups provide their members with training and information about cutting-edge technology.

Companion Websites Our Companion Websites provide valuable solutions beyond the book. Here you can download the source code, get updates and corrections, chat with other users and the author about the book, or discover links to other websites on this topic.

Need to find a bookstore? Chances are, there's a bookseller near you that carries a broad selection of PTR titles. Locate a Magnet bookstore near you at www.phptr.com.

Subscribe today! Join PHPTR's monthly email newsletter! Want to be kept up-to-date on your area of interest? Choose a targeted category on our website, and we'll keep you informed of the latest PHPTR products, author events, reviews and conferences in your interest area.

Visit our mailroom to subscribe today! **http://www.phptr.com/mail_lists**

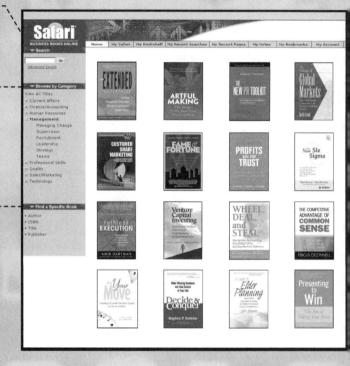